Rush Hour Recipes

HOLLY BERKOWITZ CLEGG

Also by Holly Berkowitz Clegg

A Trim & Terrific Louisiana Kitchen
Trim & Terrific American Favorites
Trim & Terrific One Dish Favorites

Nutritional Analysis by

American Institute for Cancer Research

Cover Artist and Illustrator

Emily Miletello

LCCCN: 99 96229
ISBN: 0-9610888-6-9

First Printing   February 2000
Second Printing December 2000

Printed in the USA by

WIMMER
The Wimmer Companies
Memphis
1-800-548-2537

Table of Contents

Dedication

To all the busy people who never have enough time in the day but recognize the importance of eating healthier. This book is for you!

A Note from *Holly*

Here is the perfect book for today's lifestyle as we continue to juggle the family, careers, and activities. My new cookbook offers sensible solutions for busy people who never seem to find enough hours in their day. An important role of today's parent is in "creating" healthy eating habits in their children so they will be more aware of how their food choices are affecting their health in later years. With my practical approach to cooking, a healthy meal can be prepared in thirty minutes with little effort and ingredients found in everyone's pantry. Why rely on fast food when your meals can be organized, time efficient, easily prepared and most importantly, healthy?

I was thrilled to have the opportunity to work with the American Institute for Cancer Research in this book. Their input helped me to better understand the health benefits of eating properly. Fad diets come and go, but the perfect "diet" must be a lifestyle of healthy eating. The research of the AICR proves that the inclusion of more fruits, vegetables, grains, and beans in our diet will produce positive effects on our health. I was amazed how easy it was to incorporate more veggies and fruits into my dishes. With the help of the AICR, I also discovered the variety of protective substances offered by these wonderful foods.

With my mainstream approach to cooking and my love of good food, I am providing you with the perfect balance of healthy, delicious, and yes, even easy recipes. You will recognize many of your favorite dishes, and see that they have been enhanced with ingredients that offer an abundance of flavor as well as health benefits.

I am happy to share with you the wealth of knowledge that resulted from my working with the American Institute for Cancer Research. As you flip through the pages, you'll see that a **Healthier Approach** recommendation is added to many recipes. These are suggestions offering you more options and helping ease the transition toward healthier eating patterns. You will also see **Food Facts** included with a number of recipes; these are provided to help give you a better understanding of the benefits of many foods.

The nutritional analysis of the recipes indicates that most recipes fall within the AICR recommendation of 15 and 30 percent of the total calories resulting from fat. Of course, with my sweet tooth, I had to include indulgent desserts! However, these offer a wonderful opportunity to use fruits and fruit sauces. Margarine or butter is used sparingly, often replaced with olive oil for those healthful monounsaturated fatty acids.

I suspect that one of the most popular sections of my book will be the *Mix & Match Menu Planner* which helps provide easy answers for those problem dinner nights. Also included is a *Tips & Tricks* list that helps you stock the pantry, provides substitution items and shares some inventive ideas. Finally, diabetic exchanges are tucked in at the end of the book for persons who need to keep up with that area of their daily diet.

A Note from *American Institute for Cancer Research*

The recipes in this book were developed for the busy cook who wants to enjoy a healthy diet and teach family members (especially young ones) that nutritious food can be delicious, that variety can be fun, and that cooking new things doesn't have to mean chaos in the kitchen. Best of all, these recipes highlight simple ways to incorporate into your everyday meals more fruits, vegetables and grains — foods that can significantly lower you and your family's risk of cancer.

Most of us were young children when we first heard the words, "Eat your vegetables . . . they're good for you." It's no surprise, then, to learn that these foods prevent disease. What has researchers so excited are two things: They are beginning to understand precisely how the substances within these foods work to prevent chronic illnesses like cancer and heart disease. And they are discovering the significant role that diet plays in our future health.

The American Institute for Cancer Research (AICR) translates these new findings into practical messages for Americans about the importance of a nutritious diet for good health. In 1997, AICR, along with its international affiliate, the World Cancer Research Fund, published a report called *Food, Nutrition and the Prevention of Cancer: A Global Perspective*. A panel of 16 scientists from around the world spent four years producing the report, reviewing more than 4,500 studies on diet and cancer in the process. The result was the most comprehensive report ever written on the subject of nutrition and cancer.

Included in the report are 14 diet and health recommendations for cancer prevention, which can be summarized in these simple action steps:

1. Choose a diet rich in a variety of plant-based foods.
2. Eat plenty of vegetables and fruit.
3. Maintain a healthy weight and be physically active.
4. Drink alcohol only in moderation, if at all.
5. Select foods low in fat and salt.
6. Prepare and store food safely.

And always remember . . .
Do not use tobacco in any form.

Some encouraging statistics emerged from the report as well. For instance, as many as 40 percent of all cases of cancer could be prevented through a healthy diet, exercise and maintenance of a healthy weight. And twenty percent of all cancers could be avoided if we simply ate five servings of fruits and vegetables each day.

Most Americans fall well short of this goal. Some people say it's because they don't know how to prepare healthy foods that will appeal to their families. Others think they're simply too busy to prepare them. But moving toward a healthier diet is certainly not an all-or-nothing endeavor. Small changes, like adding chopped vegetables to pasta sauce or enjoying desserts made with fresh fruits is a good way to start. The recipes and suggestions throughout this book will help make your transition to a more health-protective diet an enjoyable and satisfying one for both you and your family.

Thanks . . .

To my fun and loving husband, Mike and my precious kids, Todd, Courtney, and Haley for being my biggest success story and a ray of sunshine in my life. To Robert, for being a special part of our family.

To Jerry and Ruth, my incredible parents who I still call daily and who still spoil me with love, and Mae Mae, my other mother and my "back up," for always caring and listening enthusiastically to all my exciting opportunities.

To Ilene, my sister, who doesn't cook, yet whose advice I treasure in and out of the kitchen. To Pam (and Jim too), I can always count on you. To my family: Bart (you know your expertise), Michael and Kim, Chuck (Finky), Cannon and Cindy (cooking talk), Garney, and dearest NaNa and Papa for tasting, watching, and loving my kids.

To Al, Diane, and Anisa, I love working with you! Thanks for all your advice, expertise and great times. To the Louisiana Sweet Potato Commission for having me as your national spokesperson. I love my role as "Louisiana Yam Lady."

To Freddie, my cookbook mentor, who listens, who guides me, who shares news, and is my dear friend. Thanks to Wimmer's good work, especially the hard work of Jamaine and Ardith. To Marlene for tons of help and typing and Tammi for typing and editing – great job!

To my artist, Emily Miletello, for a job well done; you expressed my lifestyle in art!

To my best bud, Fran and Don (fish), for still being my #1 supporter about cookbooks, kids, or dog. To my buddies on and off the court (not on much lately) for their friendship, Amy (design imput), Cliffords (a long way back), Gail (sharing times), Louise (my sounding board), Lynell, Mary (soul mate) and Rob (FUN), Melanie (a special bond), Janet, and my friends . . . thanks for hanging in there with me; friends are important! To Ronnie and Louanne, fun and friendship, to Greg, for that talent with numbers, my Tulane college pals Lila, Sherri, Jolie, Les, Lauren and others: you're always included. To Renate . . . where it began so many years ago. To my Ft. Worth bridesmaids: Selma, Marcia, and Joyce– who shared recipes and time with me for so many years. To Marji–my true cooking inspiration.

To all my media and business contacts who gave me a chance and to those who are willing to give me a chance; I thank you so much!! To Katie for helping me take another step.

To Jeff, Erin, and Melanie, my new friends at the American Institute for Cancer Research Center, for working with me to make this book a resource of valuable information for everyone striving for a healthier lifestyle.

Mix & Match Menus

	STARTERS	MAIN DISHES	SIDES	SALADS & BREADS	DESSERTS
Fall Favorites	Wild Rice & Mushroom Soup Sweet Potato & Apple Soup	Chicken & Wild Rice Casserole Pork Stew Fish with Horseradish Mustard Sauce	Twiced Baked Yams Broccoli & Cauliflower with Garlic Cheese Sauce	Yam Biscuits Dinner Rolls Mixed Greens with Dressing	Sweet Potato Pecan Pie Yam Cranberry Bundt Cake
Company's Coming	Cream of Spinach & Sweet Potato Soup Crab Cakes Seafood Toast Tropical Fruity Cheese Spread	Veal Roll-Ups Trout Amandine Chicken Elegante Shrimp Stir-Fry with Toasted Pecans	Asparagus with Lemon Caper Vinaigrette Rice & Pasta Blend Herbed Carrots	Ultimate Green Salad with Balsamic Vinaigrette Sun-Dried Tomato Bread	Lemon Cheesecake with Raspberry Sauce Banana Pie with Chocolate Sauce Ultimate Coconut Cake
Greek Greats	Avocado Cucumber Soup Hummus Dip (commerically prepared)	Mediterranean Red Snapper Greek Shrimp Bake Great Greek Chicken	Herbed Carrots Rice Cheesy Eggplant Casserole	Tabbouleh Salad Tossed Salad with Feta Spinach Toast Pita Bread	Lemon Ice Ambrosia Crumble
The Big Enchilada	Mexican Layered Dip Shrimp Salsa	Shrimp Enchiladas Chicken Enchilada Casserole Pan Smoked Salmon Southwestern Style	Corny Rice	Sliced Fruit Chili Cheese Bread	Orange Raspberry Ice Cream Dessert Strawberry Cheesecake Squares
Meatless Mexican	Black Bean Chili Mango Soup	Southwestern Spinach Lasagne Southwestern Pasta Scallops with Black Beans	Canned Fat-Free Refried Beans	Black Bean & Corn Salad Orange & Walnut Green Salad	White Chocolate Bundt Cake with Raspberry Sauce Carrot Cake Banana Pudding Trifle
Leisurely Lunch	Crab Spinach Soup Frosty Strawberry Soup Crab & Avocado Mold	Chicken Salad Spinach Tortellini Salad Tuna Barley Niçoise	Tropical Couscous Salad Assorted Fruits Broccoli Salad	Sweet Potato, Apple & Walnut Muffins Banana Bread Italian Pizza Slices Spicy Tea Punch Sparkling Pineapple Lemonade	Chewy Fruity Brownies Strawberry Cheesecake Squares Espresso Brownies
Happy Holidays	Black-Eyed Pea Salsa Corn & Wild Rice Soup Tropical Fruity Cheese Spread	Maple Dijon Glazed Turkey Breast Maple Glazed Roast Pork Stuffed Tenderloin Veggie Au Gratin	Cornbread & Rice Dressing Wild Rice Stuffing Sweet Potato Cranberry Gratinee Holiday Rice Pilaf Herbed Carrots	Yam Biscuits Raspberry & Kiwi Salad with Poppyseed Dressing Black-Eyed Pea Salad	Cranberry & White Chocolate Treats Yam Cranberry Bundt Cake Sweet Potato Pecan Pie

	STARTERS	MAIN DISHES	SIDES	SALADS & BREADS	DESSERTS
Italian Ideas	Italian Pizza Slices	Italian Shrimp & Pasta Chicken Piccata Veal Scallopini Italian Pork Chops	Pesto Pasta Very Good Vermicelli	Caesar Salad Sliced Tomatoes with Fresh Mozzarella Sun-Dried Tomato Bread	Espresso Brownies Ultimate Cheesecake
Casual Dining	Shrimp Toast Crab Spinach Soup Best Black & White Bean Spread	Basil Chicken Tasty Beef Strips Veggie Paella White Spinach Pizza	Broccoli Casserole Rice Pilaf Smashed Potatoes Artichoke and Onion Couscous	Italian Puffs Super Tossed Salad	Banana Split Pie Buttermilk Brownies
Kid's Night	Creamy Potato Soup Spinach Dip	Oven Fried Chicken Spicy Topped Trout Tasty Beef Strips	Green Beans Very Good Vermicelli Potato Pizza	Tossed Salad Rolls	Slice & Bake Chocolate Chip Cookies Oatmeal Crunch Cookies Banana Split Pie
Sunday Night Dinner	Chicken Tortilla Soup Taco Soup	Easy Pot Roast Spicy Topped Trout Cheese Stuffed Manicotti Stuffed Potatoes Primavera	Scalloped Potatoes Spinach Corn Casserole Broccoli Casserole	Italian Puffs French Bread Orange & Walnut Green Salad	Pistachio Marble Cake Easy Strawberry Custard Cake
Barbecue	Black Bean & Corn Salsa Super Salsa	Barbecue Brisket Glazed Pork Tenderloin Marinated Tuna with Pineapple Salsa	Baked Beans Triple Corr Pudding Lemon Sweet Potato Casserole	Southwestern Cracked Wheat Salad Potato Salad Rice & Bean Salad Corn Bread	Buttermilk Brownies Blueberry Pineapple Delight
Winter Wonders	Corn & Wild Rice Soup Chili Boats Quick Veggie Soup	Wonderful White Chili Tasty Beef Strips Lamb Stew	Creamed Double Potatoes Barley & Mushroom Casserole Broccoli & Cauliflower with Cheese Sauce	Ultimate Green Salad with Balsamic Vinaigrette Broccoli Corn Mini Muffins	Cranberry Orange Bundt Cake Heavenly Yam Delight Fruit Crumble
Great Grilling	Super Salsa Roasted Red Peppers & Mushroom Polenta Pizza	Glazed Pork Tenderloin Stuffed Tenderloin Marinated Tuna with Pineapple Salsa	Spinach Mushroom Casserole Artichoke & Onion Risotto Broccoli Salad Sautéed Mushrooms	Black Bean & Corn Salad Sliced Tomatoes Chili Cheese Bread	Blueberry Bundt Cake Peach Cake
Summer Special	Strawberry Fruit Dip Tropical Fruit Gazpacho Marinated Shrimp	Glazed Salmon with Canteloupe Salsa Summer Veggie Pasta Basil Chicken	Squash Casserole Basic Fisotto Squash & Tomato Casserole	Spinach Salad Sliced Tomatoes & Cucumbers Tropical Couscous Salad	Easy Strawberry Cake Peachy Upside Down Cake Blueberry Pineapple Delight

BRISK BRUNCHES

Age is something that doesn't matter,
unless you are cheese.

— *Billie Burke*

Fruit Salsa Quesadillas

This picture perfect recipe was one of my most favorite brunch recipes. The fruit in the light honey glaze combined with cheese had all our mouths watering. Fill the tortillas and bake just before serving.

Quesadillas

12 (8-inch) flour tortillas, room
    temperature

1½ cups shredded part-skim
    mozzarella cheese
Fruit Salsa (recipe follows)

Preheat oven to 475 degrees. Top half of each tortilla with 2 tablespoons cheese and about ¼ cup Fruit Salsa. Fold over and place a toothpick at the end to hold the tortilla together. Place the filled tortillas on a baking sheet and bake for about 4 to 7 minutes or until lightly browned and the cheese is melted. Serve immediately.

Makes 12 servings

Fruit Salsa

1 cup chopped peeled peaches
1 quart fresh strawberries,
    hulled and diced
1 cup blueberries

1 tablespoon chopped fresh
    cilantro
1 tablespoon honey
¼ cup sliced green onions
    (scallions)

Combine the peaches, strawberries, blueberries, cilantro, honey, and green onions in a medium bowl.

Healthier Approach:
Try whole wheat tortillas or fat-free tortillas.

NUTRITIONAL INFORMATION PER SERVING

Calories	307	Saturated Fat (g)	3
Protein (g)	11	Dietary Fiber (g)	4
Carbohydrate (g)	49	Sodium (mg)	420
Fat (g)	8	Cholesterol (mg)	8
Cal. from Fat (%)	23		

Egg and Green Chili Casserole

This is a "not eggy" dish that works well
on a buffet as it easily cuts into serving portions.

2   (4-ounce) cans chopped
    green chiles, drained
8   (6-inch) flour tortillas, cut into
    1-inch strips
1   (8-ounce) package reduced-
    fat Monterey Jack cheese,
    shredded

5   large eggs
4   large egg whites
1   cup skim milk
½   teaspoon pepper
1   teaspoon ground cumin
½   teaspoon garlic powder
Salsa (optional)

Preheat the oven to 350 degrees. Coat a 2-quart baking dish with nonstick cooking spray. Layer half the chiles in the dish. Top with half the tortilla strips and then half the cheese. Repeat another layer using the remaining chiles, tortillas and cheese. In a large bowl, beat together the eggs, egg whites, milk, pepper, cumin and garlic powder and pour evenly over the casserole. Bake, uncovered, for 40 minutes or until puffy and set in the center. Let stand 10 minutes before serving. Serve with salsa, if desired.

Makes 8 servings

Healthier Approach:
To lower fat and cholesterol, 1¼ cups egg substitute can be used instead of the large eggs.

NUTRITIONAL INFORMATION PER SERVING

Calories	299	Saturated Fat (g)	5
Protein (g)	19	Dietary Fiber (g)	2
Carbohydrate (g)	29	Sodium (mg)	807
Fat (g)	11	Cholesterol (mg)	149
Cal. from Fat (%)	35		

Breakfast Bake with Spanish Sauce

The Spanish sauce is the star of this make-ahead breakfast bake.
The sauce is my dad's specialty and can be used with other dishes.
Be creative and add veggies of your choice to the bake.

Breakfast Bake

12 slices white or whole wheat bread
1 (8-ounce) package reduced-fat Cheddar cheese, shredded
5 large eggs
4 large egg whites
2½ cups skim milk

½ cup nonfat plain yogurt
1 teaspoon prepared mustard
1 teaspoon Worcestershire sauce
Salt and pepper to taste
Spanish Sauce (recipe follows)

Preheat oven to 350 degrees. Trim the crusts off the slices of bread and throw away. Coat a 3-quart oblong baking dish with nonstick cooking spray. Line the bottom of the dish with six slices of bread. Sprinkle cheese over bread layer. Top with the remaining six slices of bread. In a large bowl, blend together the eggs, egg whites, milk, yogurt, mustard, Worcestershire sauce, salt, and pepper until well mixed. Pour the egg mixture evenly over the layered bread. Cover with plastic wrap and refrigerate overnight or leave out at room temperature for 1 hour. Bake for 45 minutes to 1 hour or until puffed up, lightly browned, and cooked inside.

Makes 8 to 10 servings

Spanish Sauce

1 teaspoon minced garlic
1 large onion, chopped
3 stalks celery, chopped
1 green bell pepper, seeded and chopped
½ pound mushrooms, sliced
1 (14½-ounce) can chopped peeled tomatoes, with juice

2 (6-ounce) cans tomato paste
¼ cup water
1 teaspoon sugar
¼ teaspoon dried oregano
2 tablespoons picante sauce
2 tablespoons ketchup

In a large skillet coated with nonstick cooking spray, sauté the garlic, onion, celery, green pepper, and mushrooms until tender, about 5 to 7 minutes. Add the tomatoes, tomato paste, water, sugar, oregano, picante sauce, and ketchup. Bring to a boil, reduce the heat and cook for 30 minutes. Store in refrigerator.

Breakfast Bake *continued*

Healthier Approach:
Use "no salt added" tomato paste and canned tomatoes.

<table>
<tr><td colspan="4">NUTRITIONAL INFORMATION PER SERVING</td></tr>
</table>

Calories	253	Saturated Fat (g)	2
Protein (g)	19	Dietary Fiber (g)	5
Carbohydrate (g)	34	Sodium (mg)	820
Fat (g)	6	Cholesterol (mg)	112
Cal. from Fat (%)	21		

Coffee Punch

A wonderful brunch punch! Use your favorite flavored coffee from hazelnut to vanilla.

2 quarts brewed decaffeinated flavored coffee
1 cup sugar
1 tablespoon vanilla extract

2 cups skim milk
1 quart nonfat vanilla frozen yogurt, softened

To the brewed coffee, add the sugar and vanilla. Refrigerate until well chilled, or overnight. When ready to serve, combine the coffee mixture with the milk. Put the frozen yogurt in a punch bowl, pour the chilled coffee-milk over it. Serve immediately.

Makes 24 servings

NUTRITIONAL INFORMATION PER SERVING

Calories	71	Saturated Fat (g)	0
Protein (g)	2	Dietary Fiber (g)	0
Carbohydrate (g)	16	Sodium (mg)	33
Fat (g)	0	Cholesterol (mg)	1
Cal. from Fat (%)	0		

Bread Pudding Florentine

Delicious - a new dimension to breakfast!
Place cold dish in cold oven if using glass dish when baking.

5   large eggs
4   large egg whites
3   cups skim milk
¼   cup Dijon mustard
Salt and pepper to taste
1   (16-ounce) loaf day-old French
    bread, cut into 16 slices,
    divided
½   pound mushrooms, sliced

1   teaspoon minced garlic
1   onion, chopped
2   (10-ounce) boxes frozen
    chopped spinach, thawed
    and squeezed dry
1   tablespoon all-purpose flour
Salt and pepper to taste
1½ cups shredded reduced-fat
    Swiss cheese, divided

In a mixing bowl beat eggs and egg whites with milk, mustard, salt, and pepper; set aside. Place half the bread slices in a 13x9x2-inch baking dish coated with nonstick cooking spray. In a skillet coated with nonstick cooking spray, sauté the mushrooms, garlic, and onion until tender. Add the spinach and flour, stirring to mix well. Season with salt and pepper to taste. Spread mixture over bread. Sprinkle with 1 cup cheese. Top with remaining bread. Sprinkle with remaining ½ cup cheese. Pour egg mixture over casserole and refrigerate two hours or overnight. Bake at 350 degrees for 40 to 50 minutes or until puffed and golden.

Makes 10 to 12 servings

Food Facts:
Frozen, chopped kale is a creative alternative to spinach, and another powerhouse of nutrients.

Healthier Approach:
Use a whole grain or whole wheat French bread.

NUTRITIONAL INFORMATION PER SERVING

Calories	222	Saturated Fat (g)	2
Protein (g)	16	Dietary Fiber (g)	3
Carbohydrate (g)	29	Sodium (mg)	517
Fat (g)	5	Cholesterol (mg)	95
Cal. from Fat (%)	19		

Shrimp, Peppers, and Cheese Grits

My family cleaned their plate when I served this dish. If you are not a grits fan, the shrimp may be served over rice and used for dinner. When reheating the grits, add more milk if too thick.

1 green bell pepper, seeded and sliced	2 cups canned fat-free chicken broth
½ cup chopped tomatoes	1½ cups skim milk
1½ pounds medium shrimp, peeled	1 cup quick grits
½ cup chopped green onions (scallions)	1 cup shredded reduced-fat Cheddar cheese

In a large skillet coated with nonstick cooking spray, sauté the green pepper, tomatoes, and shrimp, cooking until the shrimp are done, about 5 to 7 minutes. Add the green onions, cooking several more minutes. Meanwhile, in a pot, bring the chicken broth and milk to a boil. Stir in the grits. Return to a boil, cover, and reduce to low heat. Cook about 5 minutes or until thickened, stirring occasionally. Stir in the cheese. Serve the shrimp over the cheese grits.

Makes 4 to 6 servings

Food Facts:

Grits are actually "hominy" or a puffed corn product. It is also known as Southern polenta. It is similar in nutritional value to other enriched grains.

NUTRITIONAL INFORMATION PER SERVING

Calories	290	Saturated Fat (g)	1
Protein (g)	34	Dietary Fiber (g)	1
Carbohydrate (g)	27	Sodium (mg)	374
Fat (g)	4	Cholesterol (mg)	177
Cal. from Fat (%)	12		

Sweet Potato Pancakes with Apple Walnut Topping

*The perfect addition for any brunch. The indulgent
Apple Walnut Topping with the Sweet Potato Pancakes makes
this a hard combination to beat. Don't let shredding the potatoes
scare you away from this delicious dish as potatoes are
easily shredded with the shredding blade of the food processor.
The Apple Walnut Topping would be a hit over vanilla ice cream.*

Pancakes

6 cups shredded peeled sweet potatoes (yams)	1 tablespoon honey
¼ cup all-purpose flour	1 large egg
½ teaspoon baking powder	2 large egg whites
⅛ teaspoon ground cinnamon	Apple Walnut Topping (recipe follows)

In a bowl, combine the shredded sweet potatoes, flour, baking powder, cinnamon, honey, egg, and egg whites with a fork until well blended. Heat a nonstick skillet coated with nonstick cooking spray, and drop about 2 tablespoons (about 3 inches each) into hot pan. Flatten slightly with the spatula and cook pancakes over medium heat until golden on both sides. Set cooked pancakes on plate and continue cooking until all pancakes are made. Serve with Apple Walnut Topping.

Note: Pancakes may be frozen or made ahead. To reheat: Place on baking sheets and bake at 450 degrees for approximately 7 to 10 minutes or until crisp.

Makes about 18 potato pancakes

Apple Walnut Topping

½ cup light brown sugar	1 tablespoon orange juice
⅓ cup chopped walnuts	⅛ teaspoon ground cinnamon
2 baking apples, peeled, cored, and thinly sliced	

In a skillet add all the ingredients and cook over a medium-high heat, stirring, until the apples are tender and the brown sugar is melted to form a syrup.

Food Facts:
A new approach to potato pancakes - sweet potatoes contain lots of beta carotene, offering more nutrition than white potatoes.

Sweet Potato Pancakes *continued*

NUTRITIONAL INFORMATION PER SERVING

Calories	130	Saturated Fat (g)	0
Protein (g)	3	Dietary Fiber (g)	2
Carbohydrate (g)	27	Sodium (mg)	32
Fat (g)	2	Cholesterol (mg)	12
Cal. from Fat (%)	11		

Berry French Toast

Use whatever fresh berries you can find or pull them
out of the freezer and enjoy this wonderful version of French toast.

5 cups mixed berries
(strawberries and
blueberries, etc.)
¾ cup sugar plus 1 tablespoon
sugar, divided
1 teaspoon cinnamon

1 large egg
4 large egg whites, beaten
1 cup skim milk
1 teaspoon vanilla extract
1 (16-ounce) loaf French bread,
sliced in 1-inch slices

Preheat oven to 350 degrees. In an oblong 2-quart casserole, put berries, ¾ cup sugar, and cinnamon. In a large bowl combine egg, egg whites, milk, and vanilla. Add bread and soak for 5 minutes turning half way through. Arrange bread in one layer over berries. Sprinkle with remaining sugar. Bake for 25 to 30 minutes or until bread is golden. Serve with berry juice and berries.

Healthier Approach:
Try whole grain French bread.

Makes 8 servings

NUTRITIONAL INFORMATION PER SERVING

Calories	289	Saturated Fat (g)	1
Protein (g)	9	Dietary Fiber (g)	4
Carbohydrate (g)	58	Sodium (mg)	397
Fat (g)	3	Cholesterol (mg)	27
Cal. from Fat (%)	8		

Apple Casserole

A great addition to any brunch when you need that something extra.

8 cups peeled and thinly sliced baking apples (about 5 large)	¼ teaspoon ground cinnamon
¾ cup sugar	¼ teaspoon ground nutmeg
⅓ cup all-purpose flour	¾ cup water

Preheat the oven to 350 degrees. Coat a 2-quart oblong glass baking dish with nonstick cooking spray, and layer the bottom with the apple slices. Mix together the sugar, flour, cinnamon, and nutmeg. Sprinkle the dry ingredients over the apples and add ¾ cup water. Cover with foil and bake for 50 to 60 minutes or until apples are tender.

Makes 6 servings

Healthier Approach:
Add ½ cup raisins. Cut sugar to ½ cup and increase cinnamon to ½ teaspoon.

NUTRITIONAL INFORMATION PER SERVING

Calories	226	Saturated Fat (g)	0
Protein (g)	1	Dietary Fiber (g)	5
Carbohydrate (g)	57	Sodium (mg)	0
Fat (g)	1	Cholesterol (mg)	0
Cal. from Fat (%)	3		

Banana Bread

Here's the perfect, yummy solution for those ripe bananas.

⅓	cup canola oil	1	teaspoon vanilla extract
1	cup dark brown sugar	2	cups all-purpose flour
2	large eggs	1	teaspoon baking soda
3	medium bananas, mashed	1	teaspoon ground cinnamon

Preheat the oven to 350 degrees. In a mixing bowl, beat together oil and brown sugar. Add eggs, bananas, and vanilla. In a separate bowl, combine flour, baking soda, and cinnamon. Gradually add the dry ingredients, stirring only until mixed. Pour batter into a 9x5x3-inch loaf pan coated with nonstick cooking spray. Bake 50 to 60 minutes or until a toothpick inserted in the center comes out clean.

Makes 12 slices

Healthier Approach:
Instead of 2 cups all-purpose flour, use 1 cup all-purpose flour, ¾ cup whole wheat flour, and ¼ cup wheat germ.

NUTRITIONAL INFORMATION PER SERVING

Calories	237	Saturated Fat (g)	1
Protein (g)	3	Dietary Fiber (g)	1
Carbohydrate (g)	41	Sodium (mg)	123
Fat (g)	7	Cholesterol (mg)	35
Cal. from Fat (%)	27		

Strawberry Bread

Another great bread made with one of my favorite fruits. Any red fruit juice can be used for cranberry-strawberry juice.

2 cups all-purpose flour	⅓ cup margarine or butter, melted
¾ cup sugar	⅓ cup cranberry-strawberry
1½ teaspoons baking powder	juice
½ teaspoon baking soda	2 teaspoons grated lemon rind
1 large egg	1½ cups strawberries, hulled and
1 large egg white	coarsely chopped

Preheat oven to 350 degrees. Coat a 9x5x3-inch loaf pan with a nonstick cooking spray. In a large bowl mix flour, sugar, baking powder, and baking soda. Beat egg and egg white slightly in a small bowl; stir in margarine, juice, and lemon rind. Add to flour mixture, stirring until well combined. Stir in berries. Pour batter into prepared pan. Bake for 50 to 60 minutes until pick inserted in bread comes out clean; cover loosely with foil if it browns too fast. Remove from pan to a wire rack to cool completely.

Makes 12 slices

Food Facts:
Strawberries offer a high antioxidant profile, as well as a healthy dose of Vitamin C.

Healthier Approach:
Experiment with 1 cup of all-purpose flour and 1 cup of whole wheat flour.

NUTRITIONAL INFORMATION PER SERVING

Calories	183	Saturated Fat (g)	1
Protein (g)	3	Dietary Fiber (g)	1
Carbohydrate (g)	30	Sodium (mg)	194
Fat (g)	6	Cholesterol (mg)	18
Cal. from Fat (%)	28		

Cranberry Yam Bread

Every time I make this bread, there is an
unbelievable response. It's a favorite.

2 large eggs, slightly beaten	1 teaspoon vanilla extract
1⅓ cups sugar	1½ cups all-purpose flour
⅓ cup canola oil	1 teaspoon ground cinnamon
1 cup mashed sweet potatoes	¼ teaspoon ground allspice
(yams) canned or cooked	1 teaspoon baking soda
fresh	1 cup chopped cranberries

Preheat oven to 350 degrees. Coat a 9x5x3-inch loaf pan with nonstick cooking spray and dust with flour. In large bowl, combine eggs, sugar, oil, yams, and vanilla. In separate bowl, combine flour, cinnamon, allspice, and baking soda. Make a well in the center. Pour yam mixture into well. Mix just until moistened. Stir in cranberries. Spoon batter into prepared loaf pan. Bake for 1 hour or until a toothpick in center in center comes out clean.

Makes 12 slices

Food Facts:
Cranberries contain a substance that appears to help prevent bacteria from adhering to the wall of the bladder. Cranberry products may help in preventing urinary tract infections.

NUTRITIONAL INFORMATION PER SERVING

Calories	222	Saturated Fat (g)	1
Protein (g)	3	Dietary Fiber (g)	1
Carbohydrate (g)	38	Sodium (mg)	119
Fat (g)	7	Cholesterol (mg)	35
Cal. from Fat (%)	28		

Lemon Raspberry Bread

Lemon and raspberries pair up perfectly in this super bread.
If using frozen raspberries, defrost before adding to batter.
Blueberries can be substituted.

¼ cup margarine or butter,
softened
⅔ cup plus ½ cup sugar, divided
1 large egg
2 large egg whites
1 tablespoon grated lemon rind
½ teaspoon vanilla extract

2¼ cups all-purpose flour
1 teaspoon baking powder
½ teaspoon baking soda
1 (8-ounce) container nonfat
lemon yogurt
1 cup raspberries
½ cup lemon juice

Preheat the oven to 350 degrees. Coat a 9x5x3-inch loaf pan with nonstick cooking spray. In a mixing bowl, cream the margarine and ⅔ cup sugar until light and fluffy. Add the egg, egg whites, lemon rind, and vanilla; beat until well blended. In another bowl, combine the flour, baking powder, and baking soda. Add the flour mixture alternately with the yogurt to the creamed mixture, beginning and ending with the flour mixture. Stir in raspberries. Pour the batter into the prepared loaf pan. Bake for 55 minutes or until a toothpick inserted in the center comes out clean. Remove from oven; place on a wire rack. Combine the remaining ½ cup sugar and lemon juice in a saucepan; bring to a boil and cook 1 minute. Remove from heat. Pierce top of bread several times with a fork or toothpick. Pour sugar mixture over bread; cool in pan 10 minutes. Remove from pan; cool completely on a wire rack.

Makes 12 servings

Food Facts:

Raspberries are a wonderful source of the powerful flavonoid ellagic acid. This substance helps protect against cancer and heart disease.

NUTRITIONAL INFORMATION PER SERVING

Calories	228	Saturated Fat (g)	1
Protein (g)	5	Dietary Fiber (g)	1
Carbohydrate (g)	43	Sodium (mg)	172
Fat (g)	5	Cholesterol (mg)	18
Cal. from Fat (%)	18		

LUNCHES ON THE RUN

STRESSED!!
(it's just desserts spelled backwards)

Frosty Strawberry Soup

This wonderful soup is like enjoying a fruit smoothie in a bowl.
Serve as a first course or a delightful lunch in hot weather.

1   quart fresh strawberries or   1½ cups buttermilk
    1 (10-ounce) package frozen   ⅛   teaspoon ground cinnamon
    strawberries, thawed   ½   cup sugar
1   cup orange juice   1   tablespoon lemon juice
2   tablespoons instant tapioca

Place berries in a food processor or blender with orange juice. Blend until smooth. In a saucepan, add tapioca to the strawberry purée. Heat, stirring constantly, until mixture comes to full boil. Cook 1 minute or until mixture thickens. Remove from heat and add buttermilk, cinnamon, sugar, and lemon juice. Refrigerate until well chilled.

Makes 6 cups

Food Facts:
The fruit in this recipe makes it a great source of Vitamin C. Buttermilk is often thought to be high in fat, but is virtually fat-free when made from skim milk.

NUTRITIONAL INFORMATION PER SERVING

Calories	149	Saturated Fat (g)	0
Protein (g)	3	Dietary Fiber (g)	2
Carbohydrate (g)	34	Sodium (mg)	66
Fat (g)	1	Cholesterol (mg)	2
Cal. from Fat (%)	6		

Mango Soup

*Mangos can also be found in jars in grocery stores
and create a wonderful, creamy, yummy soup.*

2 cups peeled and chopped mango	2 tablespoons lemon juice
1½ cups orange juice	1 teaspoon vanilla extract
3 tablespoons sugar	1 cup plain nonfat yogurt

In a food processor, combine mango, orange juice, sugar, lemon juice, vanilla and yogurt, mixing until smooth. Transfer to the refrigerator and chill.

Makes 4 cups

Food Facts:
Excellent source of beta-carotene and Vitamin C.

NUTRITIONAL INFORMATION PER SERVING

Calories	159	Saturated Fat (g)	0
Protein (g)	4	Dietary Fiber (g)	2
Carbohydrate (g)	38	Sodium (mg)	37
Fat (g)	0	Cholesterol (mg)	1
Cal. from Fat (%)	0		

Tropical Fruit Gazpacho

Here's a fruity twist to gazpacho that makes a great lunch with a sandwich. Serve in chilled mugs for a first course.

1 (11½-ounce) can tomato juice	½ cup peeled, seeded, and chopped cucumber
2 cups pineapple juice	
½ cup chopped mango	½ cup chopped green bell pepper
½ cup chopped peaches	2 tablespoons minced fresh cilantro, garnish
1 cup chopped fresh pineapple	
	Hot pepper sauce to taste

Combine all ingredients in a blender or food processor and pulse four times or until combined but not smooth. Cover and chill for at least 4 hours, if time permits.

Makes 6 (1-cup) servings

Food Facts:
Good source of Vitamin C and beta-carotene, and low in calories.

NUTRITIONAL INFORMATION PER SERVING

Calories	88	Saturated Fat (g)	0
Protein (g)	1	Dietary Fiber (g)	1
Carbohydrate (g)	22	Sodium (mg)	198
Fat (g)	0	Cholesterol (mg)	0
Cal. from Fat (%)	0		

Avocado Cucumber Soup

This creamy refreshing soup is ideal on a warm day.

1 large avocado, peeled and cut into chunks (about 1 cup)
2 cucumbers, peeled and seeded
1 cup fat-free chicken broth
1 cup evaporated skimmed milk

2 tablespoons lemon juice
Salt to taste
¼ cup chopped green onions (scallions)
½ cup chopped tomatoes

In a food processor or blender, place the avocado, cucumbers, chicken broth, evaporated milk, and lemon juice. Blend until mixture is smooth. Season to taste. Refrigerate, covered, until chilled. If soup gets too thick, add more evaporated milk or broth. Sprinkle each cup with green onions and tomatoes before serving.

Makes 4 to 6 servings

Food Facts:
The fat in avocado is monounsaturated, the "healthiest" form of fat.

NUTRITIONAL INFORMATION PER SERVING

Calories	106	Saturated Fat (g)	1
Protein (g)	5	Dietary Fiber (g)	3
Carbohydrate (g)	12	Sodium (mg)	56
Fat (g)	5	Cholesterol (mg)	2
Cal. from Fat (%)	43		

Chicken Salad

This scrumptious chicken salad is packed
full of fruit and flavor. Great for luncheons.

3 cups cooked diced chicken
  breasts
1 apple, cored and diced
1 (8-ounce) can sliced water
  chestnuts, drained
½ cup sliced green onion
  (scallions)
1 cup red grapes
1 cup green grapes

½ cup chopped celery
1 cup nonfat plain yogurt
1 tablespoon lemon juice
1 teaspoon dry mustard
1 teaspoon dried dill weed
Salt and pepper to taste
3 cups cooked wild rice

In a large bowl, combine chicken, apple, water chestnuts, green onion, grapes, and celery. In a small bowl, whisk together the yogurt, lemon juice, mustard, dill, salt, and pepper. Mix together the chicken, and wild rice. Toss with the dressing and refrigerate.

Makes 8 big servings

NUTRITIONAL INFORMATION PER SERVING

Calories	222	Saturated Fat (g)	1
Protein (g)	21	Dietary Fiber (g)	3
Carbohydrate (g)	30	Sodium (mg)	70
Fat (g)	3	Cholesterol (mg)	45
Cal. from Fat (%)	12		

Southwestern Chicken Salad

*Here's a great way to turn leftover grilled chicken
into another tasty meal that is a real winner.*

2 cups cooked chopped chicken breasts	½ cup shredded reduced-fat Cheddar cheese
1 cup chopped tomato	½ cup black beans, drained and rinsed
½ cup chopped green onions (scallions)	6 cups mixed salad greens
1 (11-ounce) can corn, drained	Southwestern Dressing (recipe follows)

In a salad bowl, mix chicken, tomato, green onions, corn, cheese, beans, and salad greens. Toss with dressing.

Southwestern Dressing

⅔ cup fat-free sour cream	1 teaspoon chili powder
½ cup picante sauce	½ teaspoon ground cumin

In a separate bowl, combine sour cream, picante sauce, chili powder, and cumin. Drizzle over salad.

Makes 6 to 8 servings

NUTRITIONAL INFORMATION PER SERVING

Calories	159	Saturated Fat (g)	1
Protein (g)	17	Dietary Fiber (g)	3
Carbohydrate (g)	18	Sodium (mg)	344
Fat (g)	3	Cholesterol (mg)	33
Cal. from Fat (%)	15		

Shrimp Pear Pasta Salad

Add the dressing just before serving; this salad absorbs the dressing. Seafood, fruit, and pasta are a combination hard to beat. Be creative and use another fruit for the pears.

Salad

8 ounces rotini (spiral) pasta	3 green onions (scallions), chopped
2 fresh pears, cored and chopped	½ pound cooked medium shrimp, peeled
½ cup red bell pepper, seeded and chopped	Dill Dijon Dressing (recipe follows)
½ cup green bell pepper, seeded and chopped	Lettuce leaves

Prepare the pasta according to the package directions omitting any oil and salt. Drain. Combine the pasta, pears, peppers, onions, and shrimp in a large bowl. Toss with the Dill Dijon Dressing. Line a salad bowl with lettuce; top with the pasta mixture and serve immediately.

Makes 6 servings

Dill Dijon Dressing

1 cup plain nonfat yogurt	½ teaspoon dried dill weed
1 tablespoon Dijon mustard	Hot pepper sauce to taste

Combine the yogurt, mustard, dill, and hot pepper sauce, blending well. Add the dressing to the salad when ready to serve.

Food Facts:
Use the dressing as a low-fat accompaniment to poached or grilled fish or chicken breast.

NUTRITIONAL INFORMATION PER SERVING

Calories	239	Saturated Fat (g)	0
Protein (g)	15	Dietary Fiber (g)	3
Carbohydrate (g)	42	Sodium (mg)	175
Fat (g)	2	Cholesterol (mg)	75
Cal. from Fat (%)	6		

Tuna and Barley Niçoise

There are several steps in preparation; however, your end result is a complete meal with a presentation that will have mouths watering. For grilled tuna, the marinade is super. The Lemon Basil Dressing perfectly complements the tuna and barley. Use fresh basil if possible. Prepare and arrange ahead, refrigerate, and drizzle dressing before serving.

Grilled Tuna

¼ cup reduced-sodium soy sauce	1 tablespoon prepared horseradish
1 tablespoon maple syrup	6 (¾-inch thick) slices tuna, approximately 2 pounds

Lemon Basil Dressing

½ cup lemon juice	¾ pound green beans
2 tablespoons olive oil	2 large hard boiled eggs, sliced
1 tablespoon fresh chopped basil	½ red onion, thinly sliced
1 teaspoon minced garlic	2 plum tomatoes, cut into wedges
4 cups water	Cracked pepper
1 cup uncooked pearl barley	Salt and pepper to taste

Combine soy sauce, maple syrup, and horseradish. Add tuna and chill one hour, turning occasionally. Remove tuna, discard marinade and grill or cook in a nonstick skillet on high heat for several minutes on each side; tuna is served rare; set aside. In a small bowl, whisk together the lemon juice, olive oil, basil, and garlic; set aside. Bring 4 cups water to a boil and add barley. Reduce heat and continue cooking until barley is done, about 45 minutes; set aside. Cook green beans in a small amount of water in microwave or on stove top until crisp tender; drain and set aside. To assemble, transfer barley to a serving platter and arrange tuna on top. Arrange green beans, eggs, onion, and tomato around tuna. Drizzle with dressing.

Makes 8 servings

Food Facts:
Barley is a whole grain, offering health protective benefits.

NUTRITIONAL INFORMATION PER SERVING

Calories	293	Saturated Fat (g)	1
Protein (g)	31	Dietary Fiber (g)	6
Carbohydrate (g)	29	Sodium (mg)	323
Fat (g)	6	Cholesterol (mg)	106
Cal. from Fat (%)	19		

Tuna Pasta Salad

This super salad takes tuna to a new level.

1   (16-ounce) package tricolored rotini
1   bunch fresh broccoli, cut into florets
2   medium tomatoes, cut into chunks
¼   cup pitted ripe olives, chopped
½   onion, cut into thin slices and rings separated

1   (12-ounce) can solid white tuna in spring water, drained
⅓   cup balsamic vinegar
¼   cup lemon juice
1   tablespoon water
2   tablespoons olive oil
2   tablespoons Dijon mustard
½   teaspoon pepper

Cook the pasta according to package directions omitting any salt and oil. Drain and combine with the broccoli florets, tomatoes, olives, onion, and tuna. Set aside. In a small bowl, combine the vinegar, lemon juice, water, olive oil, mustard, and pepper. Beat with a fork vigorously. Pour over the pasta mixture. Toss gently. Chill 2 hours. Toss gently before serving.

Makes 8 to 10 servings

Food Facts:

Tricolor pasta, or the addition of "tomato" pasta and "spinach" pasta, add visual appeal, but not nutritional extras.

NUTRITIONAL INFORMATION PER SERVING

Calories	182	Saturated Fat (g)	1
Protein (g)	13	Dietary Fiber (g)	2
Carbohydrate (g)	22	Sodium (mg)	250
Fat (g)	5	Cholesterol (mg)	15
Cal. from Fat (%)	24		

Black-Eyed Pea Salad

Works great with barbecue and, of course, on New Year's Day. A different approach to black-eyed peas and great addition to any meal.

3 tablespoons balsamic vinegar	1 tablespoon chopped parsley
2 tablespoons olive oil	or cilantro
Salt and pepper to taste	½ cup chopped red bell pepper
2 (15-ounce) cans black-eyed	½ cup chopped green bell pepper
peas, rinsed and drained	¼ cup diced red onion
⅓ cup chopped celery	1 cup chopped tomato

Stir together vinegar, olive oil, salt, and pepper; set aside. In a large bowl, mix together black-eyed peas, celery, parsley, red and green peppers, onion, and tomatoes. Toss with dressing. Cover and chill at least one hour.

Makes 4 (1-cup) servings

Food Facts:

Good source of fiber, and black-eyed peas are lower in calories than many other legumes.

NUTRITIONAL INFORMATION PER SERVING

Calories	214	Saturated Fat (g)	1
Protein (g)	11	Dietary Fiber (g)	9
Carbohydrate (g)	34	Sodium (mg)	976
Fat (g)	7	Cholesterol (mg)	0
Cal. from Fat (%)	26		

Black Bean and Corn Salad

This perfect blend of flavors make this a salad you'll repeat often.

1 (15-ounce) can black beans, drained and rinsed
1 (15-ounce) can whole kernel corn, drained
2 cups coarsely chopped tomatoes
1 bunch green onions, sliced

1 tablespoon chopped jalapeños
⅓ cup chopped fresh cilantro
¼ cup lime juice
2 tablespoons olive oil
½ teaspoon ground cumin
Salt and pepper to taste

In a bowl, combine the black beans, corn, tomatoes, green onions, jalapeños, and cilantro. In a small bowl, whisk together the lime juice, olive oil, and cumin. Toss dressing with bean mixture and season to taste with salt and pepper.

Makes 6 servings

Food Facts:
Great source of dietary fiber.

NUTRITIONAL INFORMATION PER SERVING

Calories	157	Saturated Fat (g)	1
Protein (g)	6	Dietary Fiber (g)	7
Carbohydrate (g)	25	Sodium (mg)	436
Fat (g)	6	Cholesterol (mg)	0
Cal. from Fat (%)	29		

Rice and Bean Salad

Leftover rice and canned goods from your pantry make this an easy and nutritious salad with a Southwestern flair to add to any meal.

Salad

3	cups cooked rice	2	(4-ounce) cans chopped green
1	(16-ounce) can pinto beans,		chiles, drained
	drained and rinsed	½	cup chopped red onion
1	(15-ounce) can black beans,	¼	cup chopped fresh cilantro
	drained and rinsed		Garlic Dressing (recipe follows)
1	(10-ounce) package frozen		
	green peas		

Combine the rice, pinto beans, black beans, peas, green chiles, onion, and cilantro in a large bowl; toss gently. Pour Garlic Dressing over the rice mixture and toss gently. Cover and chill overnight, if time permits.

Makes 12 to 14 servings

Garlic Dressing

⅓	cup balsamic vinegar	1	teaspoon minced garlic
¼	cup water	1	tablespoon olive oil

Combine the vinegar, water, garlic and olive oil in a jar. Cover tightly and shake vigorously.

Makes ½ cup

Food Facts:
Use this as a main dish, too. It's high in protein and dietary fiber.

NUTRITIONAL INFORMATION PER SERVING

Calories	137	Saturated Fat (g)	0
Protein (g)	5	Dietary Fiber (g)	5
Carbohydrate (g)	25	Sodium (mg)	366
Fat (g)	2	Cholesterol (mg)	0
Cal. from Fat (%)	11		

Tabbouleh Salad

Bulgur is wheat berries that have been lightly cooked, parched (dried or roasted) and cracked. It cooks very quickly. Cracked wheat (bulgur) can be found in specialty stores, health food stores, and many grocery stores. Make this terrific salad ahead to enhance flavors.

2   cups cracked wheat
2   cups finely chopped peeled
    cucumber
2   cups chopped tomatoes
    (vine ripe preferred)
1½ cups chopped parsley
    (flat leaf preferred)

1   tablespoon plus 1 teaspoon
    dried mint
3   tablespoons olive oil
⅓   cup lemon juice (use less if
    desired)
Cayenne pepper to taste
Salt and pepper to taste

In a large bowl, cover cracked wheat with twice as much hot water. Let stand for 45 minutes. Drain excess water and dry wheat as much as possible. Add cucumbers, tomato, parsley, and mint. In a small bowl, whisk together olive oil, lemon juice, cayenne, salt, and pepper. Toss with dressing.

Makes 12 to 16 servings

Food Facts:
A delicious salad that is low in sodium and high in fiber. For extra flavor, cook bulgur in broth rather than water.

NUTRITIONAL INFORMATION PER SERVING

Calories	92	Saturated Fat (g)	0
Protein (g)	3	Dietary Fiber (g)	4
Carbohydrate (g)	16	Sodium (mg)	9
Fat (g)	3	Cholesterol (mg)	0
Cal. from Fat (%)	26		

Southwestern Cracked Wheat Salad

Cracked wheat is found in health food stores or in groceries in tabbouleh mixes; discard seasoning packet and use cracked wheat only to make this fantastic Southwestern dish.

2	cups water	1	bunch green onions
1½	cups cracked wheat (bulgur)		(scallions), chopped
1	(15-ounce) can black beans,	1	tablespoon minced cilantro
	rinsed and drained	3	tablespoons orange juice
1	(10-ounce) package frozen	¼	cup lemon juice
	corn, thawed and drained	½	teaspoon ground cumin
1½	cups chopped tomato	½	teaspoon chili powder

Bring water to a boil and pour over cracked wheat in a bowl. Let set for 45 minutes or until liquid is absorbed. Drain any excess liquid. Add black beans, corn, tomato, green onions, and cilantro. In a small bowl, whisk together orange juice, lemon juice, cumin, and chili powder. Toss dressing with salad mixture. Refrigerate.

Makes 8 servings

Food Facts:

High fiber salad (and delicious). Experiment with cracked wheat as a substitute for rice in other salads and pilaf recipes.

NUTRITIONAL INFORMATION PER SERVING

Calories	175	Saturated Fat (g)	0
Protein (g)	8	Dietary Fiber (g)	9
Carbohydrate (g)	38	Sodium (mg)	175
Fat (g)	1	Cholesterol (mg)	0
Cal. from Fat (%)	5		

Couscous Salad

Couscous is very quick cooking and comes out fluffy, light, and mild in flavor. The addition of veggies and feta make this a super salad.

4 cups cooked couscous, cooled	⅓ cup crumbled feta cheese
	1 tablespoon dried oregano
⅓ cup chopped red onions	1 tablespoon olive oil
2 cups chopped tomatoes	2 tablespoons cider vinegar
1 cucumber, peeled, seeded and finely chopped	2 tablespoons lemon juice
	Dash of crushed red pepper
¼ cup chopped green onions (scallions)	flakes
	Salt and pepper to taste

Place cooled couscous in a large bowl. Add red onions, tomatoes, cucumber, green onions, and feta. In a small bowl, whisk together oregano, oil, vinegar, lemon juice, red pepper flakes, salt, and pepper. Toss with couscous mixture. Cover and refrigerate until serving.

Makes 8 servings

Healthier Approach:
Add dried chopped fruits, such as cherries, cranberries, and apricots, if desired.

NUTRITIONAL INFORMATION PER SERVING

Calories	133	Saturated Fat (g)	1
Protein (g)	4	Dietary Fiber (g)	2
Carbohydrate (g)	22	Sodium (mg)	62
Fat (g)	3	Cholesterol (mg)	4
Cal. from Fat (%)	20		

Veggie Couscous

A great, quick veggie salad that can include all your favorites.

1	(14½-ounce) can vegetable broth	1	(19-ounce) can chickpeas, rinsed and drained
1	teaspoon olive oil	2	tablespoons lemon juice
2	cups couscous	2	tablespoons balsamic vinegar
½	cup chopped red onion	½	teaspoon minced garlic
⅔	cup chopped carrots	¼	cup pine nuts, toasted
1	green bell pepper, seeded and chopped		

In a saucepan, bring vegetable broth and olive oil to a boil. Add couscous, stir, remove from heat and cover for 7 minutes. Fluff with fork and place in bowl with onion, carrots, green pepper, and chickpeas. Whisk together lemon juice, vinegar, and garlic and mix with couscous. Toss in pine nuts.

Makes 8 to 10 servings

Food Facts:

Chickpeas (garbanzo beans) are a good source of protein and iron, as well as dietary fiber.

NUTRITIONAL INFORMATION PER SERVING

Calories	218	Saturated Fat (g)	0
Protein (g)	8	Dietary Fiber (g)	5
Carbohydrate (g)	39	Sodium (mg)	298
Fat (g)	4	Cholesterol (mg)	0
Cal. from Fat (%)	15		

Tropical Couscous Salad

Couscous is easily prepared and this couscous creation will be the talk of the table.

1   cup orange juice
1   cup water
1   teaspoon olive oil
½   teaspoon ground ginger
2   cups couscous
1   (15-ounce) can mandarin oranges, drained and reserve juice

1   cup peas (if using frozen, defrost)
½   cup chopped green onions (scallions)
½   cup dried cranberries
½   teaspoon grated orange rind
Dash of cayenne pepper
1   teaspoon lemon juice
¼   cup chopped walnuts, toasted

In a saucepan, bring orange juice, water, olive oil, and ginger to a boil. Add couscous, stir, remove from heat, and cover for 7 minutes. Transfer couscous to a bowl and add oranges, peas, green onions, cranberries, and orange rind, mixing well. In a small bowl whisk together cayenne, lemon juice, and ⅓ cup of reserved mandarin juice and toss with salad. Add walnuts. Refrigerate.

Makes 8 to 10 servings

Food Facts:

Couscous is made from semolina and is a substitute for rice or pasta. Also available in whole wheat couscous, although the flavor is quite different.

NUTRITIONAL INFORMATION PER SERVING

Calories	223	Saturated Fat (g)	0
Protein (g)	7	Dietary Fiber (g)	4
Carbohydrate (g)	44	Sodium (mg)	8
Fat (g)	3	Cholesterol (mg)	0
Cal. from Fat (%)	10		

Spinach Tortellini Salad

A throw together salad with a gourmet appeal.

1 pound spinach tortellini	1 (7-ounce) jar roasted red bell
¼ cup grated Parmesan cheese	peppers, drained and chopped
1 (14-ounce) can artichoke	¼ cup red wine vinegar or cane
hearts, cut into quarters	vinegar
½ cup sliced green onions	2 tablespoons water
(scallions)	½ tablespoon olive oil
1 green bell pepper, seeded and	1 tablespoon dried basil
chopped	1 teaspoon Dijon mustard
	½ teaspoon sugar

Cook tortellini according to package directions. Drain and cool. In a large bowl, combine tortellini, Parmesan cheese, artichoke hearts, green onion, green pepper, and roasted red pepper. In a small bowl, whisk together vinegar, water, oil, basil, mustard, and sugar until well mixed. Mix with tortellini mixture. Refrigerate.

Makes 8 servings

NUTRITIONAL INFORMATION PER SERVING

Calories	165	Saturated Fat (g)	2
Protein (g)	9	Dietary Fiber (g)	2
Carbohydrate (g)	18	Sodium (mg)	428
Fat (g)	6	Cholesterol (mg)	76
Cal. from Fat (%)	34		

Greek Pasta Salad

A great choice of salad with a touch of Greek influence.
To reduce the sodium, decrease the capers.

½ cup nonfat sour cream
1 tablespoon light mayonnaise
2 tablespoons lemon juice
2 tablespoons skim milk
⅓ cup crumbled feta cheese
2 tablespoons chopped parsley
½ teaspoon dried mint
1 teaspoon dried oregano
Black pepper to taste

1 (12-ounce) package medium
   shell pasta
2 cups chopped tomatoes
2 cups peeled and diced
   cucumber
1 cup sliced green onions
   (scallions)
1 (3½-ounce) jar capers, drained

In a large bowl, combine the sour cream, mayonnaise, lemon juice, milk, feta, parsley, mint, oregano, and pepper. Cover and refrigerate. Meanwhile, prepare the pasta according to package directions, omitting oil and salt. Rinse and drain well. To the mayonnaise mixture, add the pasta, tomato, cucumber, green onions, and capers. Stir to mix well. Cover and chill to blend the flavors.

Makes 6 to 8 servings

NUTRITIONAL INFORMATION PER SERVING

Calories	217	Saturated Fat (g)	1
Protein (g)	8	Dietary Fiber (g)	2
Carbohydrate (g)	39	Sodium (mg)	367
Fat (g)	3	Cholesterol (mg)	7
Cal. from Fat (%)	12		

Broccoli Salad

Buy the already cut broccoli florets for a time saver recipe that is super to include anytime! A great way to enjoy broccoli.

4	cups broccoli florets	⅓	cup green onions (scallions)
¼	cup chopped walnuts, optional	¼	cup sugar
1	cup red seedless grapes	2	tablespoons vinegar
½	cup chopped celery	¼	cup light mayonnaise

Combine broccoli, walnuts, grapes, celery, and green onions. In a small bowl, mix together sugar, vinegar, and mayonnaise. Toss with salad. Refrigerate.

Makes 8 servings

Food Facts:

Red grapes offer a newly discovered phytochemical or cancer-protective substance called "resveratrol" - so enjoy in recipes or as a refreshing snack!

NUTRITIONAL INFORMATION PER SERVING

Calories	76	Saturated Fat (g)	1
Protein (g)	1	Dietary Fiber (g)	1
Carbohydrate (g)	13	Sodium (mg)	72
Fat (g)	3	Cholesterol (mg)	0
Cal. from Fat (%)	30		

Broccoli and Cauliflower Salad

You can always use all broccoli or cauliflower for the entire salad. Here's a recipe familiar at cafeterias that you can now enjoy at home.

4	cups broccoli florets	½	cup shredded reduced-fat Cheddar cheese
4	cups cauliflower florets		
1	cup chopped green bell pepper	¼	cup fat-free sour cream
1	cup chopped celery	¼	cup light mayonnaise
2	cups chopped tomatoes	2	tablespoons vinegar
1	(2¼-ounce) can sliced black olives, drained	1	tablespoon sugar

In a large bowl, combine broccoli, cauliflower, green pepper, celery, tomatoes, olives, and cheese. In a small bowl, mix together the sour cream, mayonnaise, vinegar, and sugar. Toss dressing with broccoli mixture.

Makes 12 to 16 servings

Food Facts:

Broccoli is also a great source of Vitamin C and antioxidant nutrients. But remember, it is variety that counts, so always include lots of other veggies.

NUTRITIONAL INFORMATION PER SERVING

Calories	48	Saturated Fat (g)	0
Protein (g)	2	Dietary Fiber (g)	2
Carbohydrate (g)	6	Sodium (mg)	100
Fat (g)	2	Cholesterol (mg)	2
Cal. from Fat (%)	36		

Potato Salad

When you need a good potato salad, you'll welcome this new twist.

3 pounds red potatoes	1½ cups fat-free sour cream
1 (8-ounce) bag shredded red cabbage	½ cup skim milk
½ cup golden raisins	1 (1-ounce) package Original Ranch salad dressing and recipe mix
1½ cups chopped apples	

Place the potatoes in a large pot and cover with water. Bring to a boil and cook until tender, but not mushy, about 20 to 30 minutes. Drain and cool. Peel potatoes and cut into chunks and place in a large bowl. Add the cabbage, raisins, and apples. In a small bowl, mix together the sour cream, milk, and Ranch dressing mix. Toss potato mixture with as much dressing as desired to coat. If you have extra, use as a dip for veggies.

Makes 12 servings

Food Facts:
Red cabbage is higher in Vitamin C than the green variety.

NUTRITIONAL INFORMATION PER SERVING

Calories	202	Saturated Fat (g)	0
Protein (g)	5	Dietary Fiber (g)	4
Carbohydrate (g)	45	Sodium (mg)	209
Fat (g)	0	Cholesterol (mg)	3
Cal. from Fat (%)	0		

Chicken Caesar Sandwich

*Here's a great idea to turn leftover chicken
or shrimp into a favorite light and delicious sandwich.*

1	(16-ounce) loaf French bread	2	tablespoons light mayonnaise
1	large head romaine lettuce, torn into pieces	1	teaspoon minced garlic
¼	cup grated Parmesan cheese	2	tablespoons lemon juice
2	cups chopped grilled or leftover chicken	1	tablespoon white vinegar
2	tablespoons fat-free sour cream	1	teaspoon Worcestershire sauce
		½	teaspoon dry mustard

Hollow out the inside of a French bread, discarding extra bread. Cut loaf in six sections to make it easier to hollow out bread; set aside. Place lettuce, Parmesan cheese, and chicken in a bowl. In a small bowl, whisk together sour cream, mayonnaise, garlic, lemon juice, vinegar, Worcestershire sauce, and mustard. Toss with lettuce mixture and stuff into each hollowed bread section.

Makes 6 sandwiches

NUTRITIONAL INFORMATION PER SERVING

Calories	299	Saturated Fat (g)	2
Protein (g)	24	Dietary Fiber (g)	3
Carbohydrate (g)	33	Sodium (mg)	580
Fat (g)	7	Cholesterol (mg)	45
Cal. from Fat (%)	20		

Shrimp Boat

*Cut in large slices for lunch or cut in thin slices for pick-ups.
This simple sandwich is hard to beat. Any leftover grilled meat
or chicken works great; I've even sautéed the shrimp in a skillet.*

1	(16-ounce) loaf French bread	½	cup shredded reduced-fat
¾	pound grilled peeled shrimp		Monterey Jack cheese
		1	large tomato, thinly sliced

Preheat oven to 350 degrees. Slice a loaf of French bread in half lengthwise. Scoop out one side. Fill with shrimp and top with cheese. Arrange tomato slices on top. Top with other half of bread. Wrap bread in foil and bake until well heated and cheese is melted, about 15 to 20 minutes. Remove from oven and slice.

Makes 10 to 12 servings

Healthier Approach:
Try using a whole wheat or whole grain loaf bread.

NUTRITIONAL INFORMATION PER SERVING

Calories	147	Saturated Fat (g)	1
Protein (g)	11	Dietary Fiber (g)	1
Carbohydrate (g)	20	Sodium (mg)	333
Fat (g)	2	Cholesterol (mg)	59
Cal. from Fat (%)	15		

White Spinach Pizza

A great quick lunch. On one side of the pizza I used cheese only on the white sauce and my youngest thought it tasted like macaroni and cheese. Be creative with your favorite toppings.

1 (10-ounce) can refrigerated pizza crust
1 cup skim milk
3 tablespoons all-purpose flour
Salt and pepper to taste
½ pound mushrooms, sliced
½ teaspoon minced garlic

3 cups fresh spinach, washed and stemmed
½ teaspoon dried basil
¼ cup crumbled feta
½ cup shredded part-skim mozzarella cheese

Preheat oven to 425 degrees. Pat crust into a round 12-inch pizza pan coated with nonstick cooking spray. Bake for 7 minutes or until crust begins to brown. In a small pot, mix together milk and flour over medium-high heat until thickened. Season with salt and pepper to taste. Spread white sauce over partially baked crust. Meanwhile, in a skillet coated with nonstick cooking spray, sauté mushrooms and garlic until tender, about 5 minutes. Add spinach, stirring until wilted. Add basil. Spread spinach mixture over white sauce. Sprinkle with feta and mozzarella cheeses. Return to oven and continue baking for 10 minutes until crust is golden brown and cheese is melted.

Makes 8 servings

Food Facts:
Substitute chopped fresh broccoli or finely chopped zucchini and red peppers, if desired.

NUTRITIONAL INFORMATION PER SERVING

Calories	152	Saturated Fat (g)	2
Protein (g)	8	Dietary Fiber (g)	1
Carbohydrate (g)	23	Sodium (mg)	316
Fat (g)	4	Cholesterol (mg)	9
Cal. from Fat (%)	21		

Spinach and Tomato Crustless Quiche

The creamy filling topped with the tomatoes made this quiche one that everyone loved and wanted seconds.

1 onion, chopped	1 (10-ounce) package frozen
½ teaspoon minced garlic	chopped spinach, thawed,
½ teaspoon dried basil	drained very well
1 (12-ounce) container low-fat	1 cup shredded reduced-fat
cottage cheese	Monterey Jack cheese
1 large egg	4 Roma (plum) tomatoes, sliced
2 large egg whites	

Preheat oven to 350 degrees. Coat a large skillet with nonstick cooking spray. Over medium-high heat, sauté the onion, stirring occasionally, until tender, about 5 minutes. Add the garlic and basil. Set aside. In a food processor or blender, purée the cottage cheese with the egg and egg whites. Add to the onion mixture. Mix in the spinach and Monterey Jack cheese. Spoon into a 9-inch pie plate coated with nonstick cooking spray. Smooth the top and bake, uncovered, for 25 minutes. Remove from oven and arrange the tomatoes in an overlapping circle on the top of the quiche. Bake, uncovered, for 20 minutes more or until a knife inserted near the center comes out clean.

Makes 6 servings

Healthier Approach:
Use nonfat cottage cheese, if desired.

NUTRITIONAL INFORMATION PER SERVING

Calories	142	Saturated Fat (g)	3
Protein (g)	17	Dietary Fiber (g)	2
Carbohydrate (g)	8	Sodium (mg)	404
Fat (g)	5	Cholesterol (mg)	56
Cal. from Fat (%)	32		

Broccoli Corn Mini Muffins

A savory muffin full of goodies that goes great with any lunch.

1 large egg
⅔ cup skim milk
1 (15-ounce) can whole kernel corn, drained
½ cup shredded reduced-fat Cheddar cheese

1 (8½-ounce) box corn muffin mix
1 (10-ounce) package frozen chopped broccoli, thawed

Preheat oven to 400 degrees. In a large bowl, mix egg and milk together. Stir in corn and cheese. Stir in muffin mix until dry ingredients are moistened. Stir in broccoli. Spoon batter into mini muffin cups coated with nonstick cooking spray or lined with papers, about two-thirds full. Bake for 12 to 15 minutes or until muffins spring back when touched.

Makes about 24 muffins

NUTRITIONAL INFORMATION PER SERVING

Calories	65	Saturated Fat (g)	1
Protein (g)	2	Dietary Fiber (g)	1
Carbohydrate (g)	11	Sodium (mg)	187
Fat (g)	2	Cholesterol (mg)	10
Cal. from Fat (%)	23		

Best Blueberry Muffins

*The hint of orange with the crumbly topping
makes this a deluxe version of blueberry muffins.*

¼ cup light brown sugar	⅓ cup sugar
1¾ cup plus 2 tablespoons all-purpose flour, divided	2 teaspoons grated orange rind
	2 tablespoons orange juice
1 tablespoon margarine, melted	¾ cup buttermilk
⅓ cup old fashioned oatmeal	3 tablespoons canola oil
1 teaspoon vanilla extract	1 large egg
2 teaspoon baking powder	1½ cups blueberries
¼ teaspoon baking soda	(fresh or frozen)

Preheat oven to 400 degrees. In a small bowl, mix together brown sugar, 2 tablespoons flour and margarine. Add the oatmeal and vanilla, stirring with a fork until well mixed; set aside. In a large bowl combine 1¾ cup flour, baking powder, baking soda, sugar and orange rind. In a small bowl combine the orange juice, buttermilk, oil, and egg. Make a well in the center of the dry ingredients and add the egg mixture, stirring just until well moistened. Stir in the blueberries. Line the muffin tins with muffin papers. Fill the muffin cups two-thirds full and sprinkle with the crumb mixture. Bake for 20 to 25 minutes or until the top springs back when touched.

Makes 12 muffins

Food Facts:
Blueberries are a good source of fiber and the phytochemical anthocyanosides that serve as antioxidants in the body to protect health.

NUTRITIONAL INFORMATION PER SERVING

Calories	181	Saturated Fat (g)	1
Protein (g)	4	Dietary Fiber (g)	1
Carbohydrate (g)	30	Sodium (mg)	145
Fat (g)	5	Cholesterol (mg)	18
Cal. from Fat (%)	26		

Sweet Potato, Apple, and Walnut Muffins

*The tartness of apples and raisins combined with the
sweetness of yams and flavorful walnuts create a moist muffin
that will quickly become one of your favorites.*

1¾ cups all-purpose flour
1½ teaspoons baking powder
1 teaspoon cinnamon
3 tablespoons canola oil
¾ cup light brown sugar
1 large egg
1 large egg white

1 (15-ounce) can sweet potatoes
  (yams), drained and mashed
½ cup skim milk
1¾ cups chopped peeled baking
  apples
⅓ cup chopped walnuts
⅓ cup golden raisins

Preheat oven to 400 degrees. In a bowl, mix together flour, baking powder, and cinnamon; set aside. In another bowl, mix together the oil, brown sugar, egg, egg white, mashed yams, and milk until well mixed. Make a well in the center of the dry ingredients and add yam mixture, stirring until moistened. Do not overmix. Fold in the apples, walnuts, and raisins. Spoon batter into paper lined or coated muffin tins, filling about three-fourths full. Bake for 20 to 25 minutes or until done.

Makes approximately 18 muffins

Food Facts:
Sweet potatoes offer a healthy dose of beta-carotene.

NUTRITIONAL INFORMATION PER SERVING

Calories	160	Saturated Fat (g)	0
Protein (g)	3	Dietary Fiber (g)	1
Carbohydrate (g)	28	Sodium (mg)	73
Fat (g)	4	Cholesterol (mg)	12
Cal. from Fat (%)	22		

Bran Muffins

The perfect make ahead muffin. Prepare batter and keep in refrigerator until ready to use; hot muffins instantly.

4 cups wheat bran flake cereal with raisins	½ cup sugar
1½ cups all-purpose flour	½ cup light brown sugar
1 cup whole wheat flour	2 cups buttermilk
1½ teaspoons baking soda	¼ cup canola oil
	2 large eggs

In a large bowl, combine cereal, all-purpose flour, wheat flour, baking soda, sugar, and brown sugar. In another bowl, mix buttermilk, oil, and eggs; add to dry ingredients, stirring just until moistened. Cover and refrigerate (dough best if chilled). Preheat oven to 400 degrees. Spoon batter into muffin tins coated with nonstick cooking spray, filling about three-fourths full. Bake 15 to 17 minutes or until golden.

Makes 2 dozen muffins

Healthier Approach:
Add finely diced chopped apricots or other ingredients.

NUTRITIONAL INFORMATION PER SERVING

Calories	144	Saturated Fat (g)	0
Protein (g)	4	Dietary Fiber (g)	2
Carbohydrate (g)	27	Sodium (mg)	167
Fat (g)	3	Cholesterol (mg)	18
Cal. from Fat (%)	19		

Sparkling Pineapple Lemonade

Serve with a slice of lemon and/or pineapple in each glass.

⅓ cup sugar
½ cup lemon juice
1½ cups water

3½ cups pineapple juice
3½ cups club soda
Lemon, sliced

Combine sugar, lemon juice, and water in a large pitcher; stir until sugar is completely dissolved. Stir in pineapple juice and club soda. Serve over ice with lemon slices.

Makes about 10 (1-cup) servings

NUTRITIONAL INFORMATION PER SERVING

Calories	78	Saturated Fat (g)	0
Protein (g)	0	Dietary Fiber (g)	0
Carbohydrate (g)	20	Sodium (mg)	18
Fat (g)	0	Cholesterol (mg)	0
Cal. from Fat (%)	0		

Spicy Tea Punch

Float slices of orange on top when serving.

3 cups boiling water
6 regular size tea bags
¼ teaspoon ground cinnamon
¼ teaspoon ground nutmeg
¾ cup sugar

3 cups cranberry juice cocktail
2 cups water
1 cup orange juice
⅓ cup lemon juice

Pour 3 cups boiling water over tea, cinnamon, and nutmeg. Cover and steep 5 minutes. Remove tea bags. Add sugar and stir until dissolved. Cool. Add cranberry juice, water, orange juice, and lemon juice. Chill. Serve over ice cubes.

Makes about 12 (1-cup) servings

Healthier Approach:
Decrease sugar in accordance with taste.

NUTRITIONAL INFORMATION PER SERVING

Calories	95	Saturated Fat (g)	0
Protein (g)	0	Dietary Fiber (g)	0
Carbohydrate (g)	24	Sodium (mg)	2
Fat (g)	0	Cholesterol (mg)	0
Cal. from Fat (%)	0		

Espresso Brownies

These rich chocolate brownies are one of my very favorites.
Serve with raspberries or strawberries for a true delight.

½ cup margarine
1 cup sugar
1 large egg
1 large egg white
1 teaspoon vanilla extract
1¼ cups all-purpose flour

⅓ cup cocoa
1 tablespoon instant espresso
   coffee powder (see note below)
1 teaspoon baking powder
⅓ cup semisweet chocolate chips

Preheat oven to 350 degrees. In a large mixing bowl, beat the margarine, sugar, egg, egg white, and vanilla until light and fluffy. Combine the flour, cocoa, espresso powder, and baking powder. Gradually add the dry ingredients, mixing well. Stir in chocolate chips. Pour batter into a 9x9x2-inch pan coated with nonstick cooking spray. Bake for 20 to 25 minutes or until toothpick inserted comes out clean.

Note: Instant espresso coffee is found in the grocery store where you find coffee. I usually don't like to make you purchase unusual ingredients but you'll use this instant espresso often to make these incredible brownies over and over again.

Makes approximately 30 brownies

Healthier Approach:
Most of us need an indulgence every once in a while...so watch your portion size and enjoy.

NUTRITIONAL INFORMATION PER SERVING

Calories	86	Saturated Fat (g)	1
Protein (g)	1	Dietary Fiber (g)	1
Carbohydrate (g)	12	Sodium (mg)	62
Fat (g)	4	Cholesterol (mg)	7
Cal. from Fat (%)	40		

Chewy Fruity Blonde Brownies

The tart fruit with the caramel brownie makes this a hit.
For the kids, use chocolate-coated candies in place of the fruit.

½ cup margarine or butter, melted	2 cups all-purpose flour
1 cup light brown sugar	2 teaspoons baking powder
1 cup dark brown sugar	1 teaspoon vanilla extract
1 large egg	½ cup chopped dried apricots
1 large egg white	½ cup chopped dried
¼ cup orange juice	cranberries

Preheat oven to 325 degrees. In a large bowl, mix together melted margarine and light and dark brown sugars; stir well. Add egg, egg white, and orange juice, mixing well. Mix flour and baking powder and add to mixture. Add vanilla. Stir in dried fruit. Bake in a 13x9x2-inch pan coated with nonstick cooking spray for 20 to 25 minutes. Cut into squares.

Makes 36 brownies

Healthier Approach:
Substitute 1 cup whole wheat flour for half of the all-purpose flour. Add ¼ cup wheat germ to the batter.

NUTRITIONAL INFORMATION PER SERVING

Calories	107	Saturated Fat (g)	0
Protein (g)	1	Dietary Fiber (g)	0
Carbohydrate (g)	20	Sodium (mg)	69
Fat (g)	3	Cholesterol (mg)	6
Cal. from Fat (%)	23		

Carrot Cake

A carrot cake with a cream cheese frosting is hard to beat!

Cake

2 cups all-purpose flour	3 large egg whites
1 teaspoon baking powder	⅓ cup canola oil
1 teaspoon baking soda	½ cup light brown sugar
1 teaspoon ground cinnamon	½ cup sugar
¼ teaspoon ground nutmeg	¼ cup light corn syrup
3 cups shredded carrots	1 teaspoon vanilla extract
1 large egg	

Preheat oven to 350 degrees. In a bowl, combine flour, baking powder, baking soda, cinnamon, and nutmeg; set aside. In a mixing bowl, beat carrots, egg, egg whites, oil, brown sugar, sugar, corn syrup and vanilla. Gradually add dry ingredients, mixing well. Pour batter into a 13x9x2-inch baking pan coated with nonstick cooking spray and bake for 30 minutes or until a toothpick inserted comes out clean. Cool.

Makes 24 squares

Cream Cheese Frosting

2 tablespoons margarine	1 teaspoon coconut extract
1 (8-ounce) package fat-free cream cheese	2½ cups confectioners' sugar

Cream margarine and cream cheese. Add coconut extract and confectioners' sugar. Blend until smooth.

Healthier Approach:
Substitute 1 cup whole wheat pastry flour for 1 cup all-purpose flour. (For a denser product, use regular whole wheat flour.)

NUTRITIONAL INFORMATION PER SERVING

Calories	177	Saturated Fat (g)	1
Protein (g)	3	Dietary Fiber (g)	1
Carbohydrate (g)	32	Sodium (mg)	158
Fat (g)	4	Cholesterol (mg)	10
Cal. from Fat (%)	22		

Blueberry Bundt Cake

When blueberries are in season, this moist bundt cake
with a touch of lemon sure hits the spot.

2½ cups all-purpose flour	2 large eggs
1 teaspoon baking soda	1 teaspoon vanilla extract
1 teaspoon baking powder	1 cup buttermilk
1 tablespoon grated lemon rind	1 cup fat-free sour cream
½ cup margarine or butter,	2 cups fresh blueberries
softened	1 cup confectioners' sugar
1 cup sugar	1 tablespoon skim milk
½ cup light brown sugar	1 tablespoon lemon juice

Preheat oven to 350 degrees. Combine flour, baking soda, baking powder, and lemon rind. In a mixing bowl, cream margarine, sugar, and brown sugar. Beat in eggs and vanilla. Add dry ingredients alternately with buttermilk and sour cream, beating well after each addition. Stir in blueberries. Pour batter into a 10-cup bundt pan coated with nonstick cooking spray. Bake for 1 hour or until toothpick inserted comes out clean. Cool thoroughly in pan. Remove. Combine confectioners' sugar, milk, and lemon juice. Drizzle over cake.

Makes 16 servings

Healthier Approach:
Top with strawberries and raspberries mixed with additional blueberries.

NUTRITIONAL INFORMATION PER SERVING

Calories	264	Saturated Fat (g)	1
Protein (g)	5	Dietary Fiber (g)	1
Carbohydrate (g)	47	Sodium (mg)	227
Fat (g)	7	Cholesterol (mg)	28
Cal. from Fat (%)	23		

Peach Cake

A pound cake with a peach personality.

Cake

2	cups sugar	1	cup buttermilk
½	cup margarine	2	cups all-purpose flour
2	large eggs	2	cups mashed peaches
2	large egg whites		Glaze (recipe follows)
2	teaspoons baking soda		

Preheat oven to 350 degrees. In a mixing bowl, mix sugar, margarine, eggs, and egg whites until creamy. Dissolve soda into buttermilk and add to creamed mixture. Gradually add flour to mixture. Add peaches, mixing well. Pour into a tube pan coated with nonstick cooking spray. Bake for 1 hour or until a toothpick inserted comes out clean. Cool, remove from pan, and pour Glaze over cake.

Makes 16 servings

Glaze

1	cup confectioners' sugar	1-2 tablespoons lemon juice

Mix confectioners' sugar with enough lemon juice to make a glaze consistency. Drizzle over cake.

Healthier Approach:
Top each serving with fresh sliced peaches or eliminate glaze and top with sliced peaches and a bit of puréed raspberries.

NUTRITIONAL INFORMATION PER SERVING

Calories	263	Saturated Fat (g)	1
Protein (g)	4	Dietary Fiber (g)	1
Carbohydrate (g)	48	Sodium (mg)	267
Fat (g)	7	Cholesterol (mg)	27
Cal. from Fat (%)	23		

Strawberry Cheesecake Squares

A cheesecake, everyone's favorite, with a fruit glaze makes an attractive and tasty pick-up.

1 cup all-purpose flour	½ cup fat-free ricotta cheese
½ cup old-fashioned oatmeal	¼ cup sugar
⅓ cup confectioners' sugar	1 (10-ounce) package frozen
3 tablespoons margarine or	strawberries in syrup, thawed
butter	½ cup canned crushed
3 tablespoons orange juice,	pineapple in juice, undrained
divided	1 tablespoon cornstarch
1 (8-ounce) package light cream cheese	

Preheat oven to 350 degrees. In a bowl, combine flour, oatmeal, and confectioners' sugar. Cut in margarine until mixture is crumbly. Stir in 2 tablespoons orange juice. Press into the bottom of a 9-inch square pan coated with nonstick cooking spray. Bake for 10 to 12 minutes. In a mixing bowl, beat cream cheese, ricotta, sugar, and remaining 1 tablespoon orange juice until smooth. Spread over crust. In a saucepan, combine thawed strawberries, pineapple, and cornstarch, stirring until smooth. Cook over medium heat, stirring constantly, until thickened. Spoon over cheese mixture. Return to oven and bake for 15 minutes or until cheese layer is set: cool completely. Refrigerate and cut into squares.

Makes 16 squares

Healthier Approach:
Top with whole, fresh strawberries.

NUTRITIONAL INFORMATION PER SERVING

Calories	121	Saturated Fat (g)	1
Protein (g)	3	Dietary Fiber (g)	1
Carbohydrate (g)	19	Sodium (mg)	83
Fat (g)	4	Cholesterol (mg)	5
Cal. from Fat (%)	27		

RUSH HOUR DINNERS

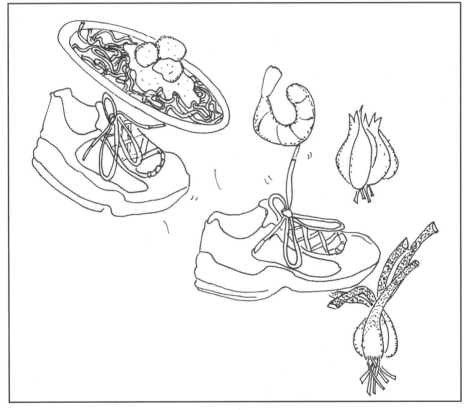

*"Any mother could perform the jobs of several
air-traffic controllers with ease."*

*Air traffic controller skills would look good on a resume.

— Lisa Alther

Creamy Potato Soup

When the potatoes are puréed, they give the soup great body and creaminess, but no added fat. For the deluxe version, serve with reduced-fat shredded Cheddar cheese and a dollop of fat-free sour cream.

2 tablespoons olive oil	4 cups peeled, diced potatoes (about 3 large)
1 cup chopped onion	1 cup evaporated skimmed milk
2 large cloves garlic, minced	Salt and pepper to taste
3 tablespoons all-purpose flour	½ cup sliced green onions (scallions)
2 (16-ounce) cans fat-free chicken broth	

Heat oil in a large pot over medium heat. Add onion and garlic and sauté until tender, about 5 minutes. Lower the heat and add the flour, stirring until smooth. Cook 1 minute, stirring constantly. Gradually add the broth, stirring constantly. Add the potatoes. Bring to a boil. Cover, reduce heat, and simmer for 20 minutes, stirring occasionally, or until the potatoes are tender. Transfer the mixture to a blender or food processor and blend until smooth, in batches if necessary. Return to the pot, stir in the evaporated milk, season to taste with salt and pepper, and heat thoroughly. Garnish with green onions.

Makes 6 to 8 servings

NUTRITIONAL INFORMATION PER SERVING

Calories	145	Saturated Fat (g)	1
Protein (g)	7	Dietary Fiber (g)	2
Carbohydrate (g)	21	Sodium (mg)	123
Fat (g)	4	Cholesterol (mg)	1
Cal. from Fat (%)	22		

Mushroom Barley Soup

SOUPS

A savory soup that hits the spot on a cool night.
For a fast version, use quick cooking barley.

1	teaspoon minced garlic	1	(8-ounce) can tomato sauce
1	onion, chopped	8	cups beef or vegetable broth
2	carrots, chopped	¾	cup medium pearl barley
½	pound sliced mushrooms		Salt and pepper to taste
1	cup shiitake mushrooms, sliced		

In a large pot coated with nonstick cooking spray, sauté the garlic, onion, carrot, and mushrooms until tender. Add tomato sauce and broth. Bring to a boil and add barley. Reduce heat, cover and cook for 1 hour or until barley is done. Season to taste with salt and pepper. Add more water, if needed.

Makes 8 servings

Healthier Approach:
Use "low-salt" broth or homemade broth to lower sodium level.

Food Facts:
Barley is a whole grain, high in fiber.

NUTRITIONAL INFORMATION PER SERVING

Calories	126	Saturated Fat (g)	0
Protein (g)	8	Dietary Fiber (g)	5
Carbohydrate (g)	24	Sodium (mg)	1181
Fat (g)	0	Cholesterol (mg)	0
Cal. from Fat (%)	0		

Wild Rice and Mushroom Soup

A wonderful, hearty soup that is a meal itself.
You can always add leftover turkey or chicken if you prefer.

1   (6-ounce) box long-grain and
    wild rice
1   onion, chopped
1   pound variety sliced
    mushrooms
½   cup chopped green bell pepper

⅓   cup all-purpose flour
4   cups canned fat-free chicken
    broth
1   (12-ounce) can evaporated
    skimmed milk

Cook rice according to package directions; set aside. In a pot coated with nonstick cooking spray, sauté the onion, mushrooms, and green peppers until tender. Add flour, stirring. Gradually stir in chicken broth and heat until boiling. Add evaporated milk and rice. Season to taste. Add more chicken broth if too thick.

Makes 8 (1-cup) servings

NUTRITIONAL INFORMATION PER SERVING

Calories	161	Saturated Fat (g)	0
Protein (g)	10	Dietary Fiber (g)	2
Carbohydrate (g)	30	Sodium (mg)	433
Fat (g)	1	Cholesterol (mg)	2
Cal. from Fat (%)	3		

Quick Veggie Soup

Any combination of cooked leftover vegetables may be substituted for the corn and carrots. This is a hearty and mild-flavored favorite soup for kids.

1 onion, chopped	1 small bay leaf
1 teaspoon minced garlic	1 cup sliced carrots
1 (16-ounce) can tomato purée	1 (10-ounce) package frozen corn
4 cups water	1 (10-ounce) package frozen green peas
Salt and pepper to taste	⅓ cup rice
1 tablespoon light brown sugar	
1 tablespoon Worcestershire sauce	

In a large pot, sauté onions, and garlic until done, about 7 minutes. Add the tomato purée, water, salt and pepper, brown sugar, Worcestershire sauce, bay leaf, carrots and corn. Bring to a boil and simmer for about 20 minutes. Add the peas and rice, cover, and simmer about 40 to 45 minutes longer or until the rice is done. Remove the bay leaf before serving. Add more water if needed while cooking to keep a soup consistency.

Makes 6 servings

Healthier Approach:
Add a small can of garbanzo beans, if desired.

NUTRITIONAL INFORMATION PER SERVING

Calories	138	Saturated Fat (g)	0
Protein (g)	5	Dietary Fiber (g)	5
Carbohydrate (g)	31	Sodium (mg)	350
Fat (g)	0	Cholesterol (mg)	0
Cal. from Fat (%)	0		

Sweet Potato and Apple Soup

*By blending sweet potatoes and apples with a touch of
ginger and curry, you have an incredibly flavored soup that
leaves a lasting impression. The toasty walnuts add the
perfect finishing touch to make this a perfect fall soup.*

½	cup chopped onions	½	teaspoon ground ginger
4	cups peeled and chopped	½	teaspoon ground curry
	sweet potatoes (yams)	1	tablespoon honey
2	cups peeled, cored, and	1	cup skim milk
	chopped baking apples	⅓	cups chopped walnuts, toasted
2	cups fat-free canned chicken		
	broth		

In a nonstick pot coated with nonstick cooking spray, sauté the onions until
tender. Add the sweet potatoes, apples, chicken broth, ginger, curry, and honey.
Bring the mixture to a boil. Reduce heat, cover, and simmer until the potatoes
are tender, approximately 25 minutes. Transfer to a food processor and purée
until smooth. Return to pot; stir in the milk until blended. Sprinkle each serving
with toasted walnuts.

Makes 5 cups

*Note: Make ahead and refrigerate. To reheat, add more milk if needed
to get soup consistency.*

Food Facts:
Sweet potatoes offer an excellent source of beta-carotene.

NUTRITIONAL INFORMATION PER SERVING

Calories	238	Saturated Fat (g)	0
Protein (g)	7	Dietary Fiber (g)	6
Carbohydrate (g)	53	Sodium (mg)	110
Fat (g)	0	Cholesterol (mg)	1
Cal. from Fat (%)	0		

Cream of Spinach and Sweet Potato Soup

*Spinach and sweet potatoes join together to produce
this sensational, creamy, rich-flavored soup.*

1 cup chopped onion	3 cups diced and peeled sweet
½ cup chopped celery	potatoes (yams)
1 red bell pepper, seeded and	1 (10-ounce) bag fresh spinach
chopped	leaves, stemmed and
2 tablespoons minced garlic	coarsely chopped
1 cup all-purpose flour	2 cups skim milk
3 (16-ounce) cans fat-free	½ cup sliced green onion stems
chicken broth	(scallions)
	Salt and pepper to taste

In a large heavy pot coated with nonstick cooking spray over a medium-high heat, cook the onion, celery, red bell pepper and garlic until the vegetables are tender, about 5 to 7 minutes. Stir in the flour and gradually add the chicken broth, whisking until the soup is blended. Add the sweet potatoes and bring to a boil, reduce the heat and cook approximately 20 minutes or until the potatoes are very tender. Add the spinach, milk, green onion stems, salt, and pepper, cooking until spinach is wilted and soup well heated and thickened, about 5 minutes.

Makes 8 servings

Food Facts:
Spinach and sweet potatoes together - a powerhouse of beta-carotene and folate.

NUTRITIONAL INFORMATION PER SERVING

Calories	208	Saturated Fat (g)	0
Protein (g)	11	Dietary Fiber (g)	4
Carbohydrate (g)	40	Sodium (mg)	197
Fat (g)	1	Cholesterol (mg)	1
Cal. from Fat (%)	2		

Southwestern Chicken Soup

*Lots of times I boil the chicken in seasoned water with
onion and celery until the chicken is done. Then, I have broth
and cooked chicken for this recipe, and you don't need the canned
broth. If desired, serve with shredded Cheddar cheese.*

1   medium red onion, chopped
½   teaspoon minced garlic
2   (14¼-ounce) cans fat-free
    chicken broth
1   (15½-ounce) can great
    Northern beans, rinsed and
    drained

1   (4-ounce) can chopped green
    chiles
2   teaspoons dried oregano
1   teaspoon ground cumin
3   cups cooked, chopped
    chicken
1   cup frozen corn

In a large pot coated with nonstick cooking spray, sauté the onion and garlic
until tender, about 5 minutes. Add the chicken broth, beans, chiles, oregano,
and cumin. Bring to a boil; reduce heat. Cover and simmer for 15 minutes. Add
the chicken and corn. Cover and cook for 10 minutes more or until heated
through.

Makes 6 servings

Healthier Approach:
*Add ½ can black beans for additional variety and fiber. Use chicken
breast only.*

NUTRITIONAL INFORMATION PER SERVING

Calories	238	Saturated Fat (g)	2
Protein (g)	29	Dietary Fiber (g)	5
Carbohydrate (g)	21	Sodium (mg)	652
Fat (g)	6	Cholesterol (mg)	59
Cal. from Fat (%)	21		

Chicken Tortilla Soup

An excellent choice for a family favorite. All my kids loved this recipe and everyone included their choice of condiments. The tortilla strips are a winner and we made extra of these for munchies.

Soup

1   onion, chopped
1   teaspoon minced garlic
4   cups canned fat-free chicken broth
1   (28-ounce) can tomatoes, chopped
1   (10¾-ounce) can tomato purée

1½ pounds boneless skinless chicken breasts, cut into chunks
1   tablespoon chili powder
1   teaspoon ground cumin
2   tablespoon lime juice
1   (16-ounce) bag frozen corn

Tortilla Strips and Condiments

4   (6-inch) flour tortillas, baked
1   cup reduced-fat shredded Cheddar cheese

½   cup sliced green onions (scallions)
1   small avocado, peeled and diced, optional

In a large pot coated with nonstick cooking spray, sauté the onion and garlic until tender, about 5 minutes. Add the chicken broth, tomatoes, tomato purée, chicken, chili powder, cumin, and lime juice and bring mixture to a boil. Lower heat and continue cooking until chicken is done, about 15 to 20 minutes. Add corn and continue cooking 5 more minutes. Serve with tortilla strips and condiments.

To make tortilla strips, while soup is cooking, preheat oven to 350 degrees. Cut tortillas into ½-inch wide strips. Coat a baking sheet with nonstick cooking spray and lay strips over sheet. Bake 15 to 20 minutes or until lightly browned. Strips may be stored in zip lock bags or frozen.

Makes 6 to 8 servings

Healthier Approach:
Try whole wheat tortillas. Use reduced-sodium chicken broth, if desired.

NUTRITIONAL INFORMATION PER SERVING

Calories	259	Saturated Fat (g)	1
Protein (g)	22	Dietary Fiber (g)	4
Carbohydrate (g)	36	Sodium (mg)	618
Fat (g)	4	Cholesterol (mg)	28
Cal. from Fat (%)	13		

Taco Soup

*This unbelievably wonderful and simple soup is the perfect
solution for the night you don't want to cook. Just open the cans
and you will be the star of the kitchen. For a less spicy soup,
substitute 1 (14½-ounce) can chopped tomatoes with
juice for diced tomatoes and green chiles.*

1	pound ground sirloin	1	(15-ounce) can kidney beans with juice
2	(10-ounce) cans diced tomatoes and green chiles with juice	1	(4½-ounce) can chopped green chiles, undrained
2	(11-ounce) cans whole kernel corn with juice	1	(1-ounce) package original ranch salad dressing mix
1	(15-ounce) can pinto beans with juice	1	(1¼-ounce) package taco seasoning mix

In a large pot, over a medium-high heat, cook the ground sirloin until done,
about 5 to 7 minutes. Drain any excess grease. Add the tomatoes and green
chiles, corn, pinto beans, kidney beans, green chiles, ranch dressing mix, and
taco seasoning mix. Bring to a boil; reduce the heat and cook 5 to 10 minutes
or until well heated. If soup is too thick, add water.

Makes 6 servings

Healthier Approach:
*Try ground turkey breast in place of ground sirloin for a low fat protein
substitute. To lower sodium, use "no salt added" canned products and
rinse beans before adding.*

NUTRITIONAL INFORMATION PER SERVING

Calories	387	Saturated Fat (g)	2
Protein (g)	32	Dietary Fiber (g)	9
Carbohydrate (g)	44	Sodium (mg)	1628
Fat (g)	8	Cholesterol (mg)	63
Cal. from Fat (%)	20		

Crab Spinach Soup

Whip this wonderful soup together in minutes.
Leave the crab out for a delicious Cream of Spinach Soup.

2 (10-ounce) packages frozen chopped spinach, thawed
1 (14½-ounce) can fat-free chicken broth
1 tablespoon margarine
1 cup chopped onion
½ pound sliced mushrooms
½ cup chopped green bell peppers
3 tablespoons all-purpose flour
2 (12-ounce) cans evaporated skimmed milk
1 teaspoon Worcestershire sauce
1 bay leaf
¼ teaspoon dried thyme
Salt and pepper to taste
1 pound white crabmeat, picked for shells

In a food processor, process spinach and broth until smooth, In a saucepan, melt margarine and sauté onions, mushroom, and green peppers. Add flour and gradually stir in evaporated milk, cooking until mixture comes to a boil. Lower heat and cook until thick. Stir in spinach mixture, Worcestershire sauce, bay leaf, thyme, salt, and pepper; continue cooking 10 minutes or until spinach is tender. Before serving, add crabmeat and remove bay leaf.

Makes 8 (1-cup) servings

NUTRITIONAL INFORMATION PER SERVING

Calories	209	Saturated Fat (g)	1
Protein (g)	22	Dietary Fiber (g)	4
Carbohydrate (g)	19	Sodium (mg)	521
Fat (g)	6	Cholesterol (mg)	56
Cal. from Fat (%)	24		

Strawberry and Kiwi Mixed Green Salad with Poppy-Sesame Dressing

The poppy and sesame seeds in the dressing make this a sensational salad. This dressing would be great over fruit salad, too.

8	cups mixed greens (Bibb, red leaf, spinach)	1	tablespoon sesame seeds
1	pint strawberries, sliced	1	tablespoon minced onion
3	kiwis, peeled and sliced	⅓	cup cane or raspberry vinegar
⅓	cup sugar	¼	cup balsamic vinegar
1	tablespoon poppy seeds	2	tablespoons olive oil

In a large bowl, mix together the greens, strawberries, and kiwi. In a small bowl combine the sugar, poppy seeds, sesame seeds, onion, cane vinegar, balsamic vinegar, and olive oil. Refrigerate dressing until ready to use. When ready to toss salad, add dressing gradually and serve immediately.

Makes 6 to 8 servings

Food Facts:
A colorful and tasty source of Vitamin C. Substitute fresh raspberries for variety.

NUTRITIONAL INFORMATION PER SERVING

Calories	121	Saturated Fat (g)	1
Protein (g)	2	Dietary Fiber (g)	3
Carbohydrate (g)	19	Sodium (mg)	17
Fat (g)	5	Cholesterol (mg)	0
Cal. from Fat (%)	34		

Caesar Salad

*The creamy full flavored dressing will make this
your favorite version for this popular salad.*

2 tablespoons lemon juice	2 tablespoons olive oil
½ tablespoon minced garlic	¼ cup fat-free sour cream or
1 teaspoon Worcestershire	plain yogurt
sauce	1 bunch romaine lettuce, washed,
Black pepper (freshly ground	drained, and torn into pieces
preferred)	3 tablespoons grated Parmesan
1 teaspoon Dijon mustard	cheese

In a small bowl whisk together the lemon juice, garlic, Worcestershire sauce, pepper, mustard, and olive oil until blended. Add sour cream, mixing well. In a large salad bowl combine lettuce and cheese. Toss with the dressing.

Makes 6 servings

NUTRITIONAL INFORMATION PER SERVING

Calories	71	Saturated Fat (g)	1
Protein (g)	3	Dietary Fiber (g)	1
Carbohydrate (g)	3	Sodium (mg)	99
Fat (g)	6	Cholesterol (mg)	3
Cal. from Fat (%)	67		

Ultimate Green Salad with Balsamic Vinaigrette

*Whenever I make this salad, it steals the show.
A great way to enjoy fruit, and the honey in the dressing
complements the salad to perfection. Store the extra
dressing in the refrigerator for later use.*

Salad

1 pound mesclun mix	1 (8-ounce) can mandarin
¼ cup crumbled blue cheese	oranges, drained
crumbs	¼ cup chopped pecans, toasted
1 cup fresh strawberries	Balsamic Vinaigrette
	(recipe follows)

In a large bowl, mix together the mesclun, blue cheese, strawberries, mandarin oranges, and pecans. Toss with Balsamic Vinaigrette before serving.

Makes 6 servings

NUTRITIONAL INFORMATION PER SALAD SERVING

Calories	90	Saturated Fat (g)	1
Protein (g)	3	Dietary Fiber (g)	2
Carbohydrate (g)	9	Sodium (mg)	98
Fat (g)	5	Cholesterol (mg)	4
Cal. from Fat (%)	49		

Balsamic Vinaigrette

3 tablespoons olive oil	½ cup honey
½ cup balsamic vinegar	2 tablespoons Dijon mustard
1 teaspoon dried oregano	Salt and pepper to taste
1 teaspoon minced garlic	

In a bowl, combine the olive oil, vinegar, oregano, garlic, honey and mustard. Season with salt and pepper and whisk to blend.

Makes about 10 (2-tablespoon) servings

Food Facts:
Strawberries offer ellagic acid, a powerful antioxidant being studied for its health protective properties.

NUTRITIONAL INFORMATION PER DRESSING SERVING

Calories	100	Saturated Fat (g)	1
Protein (g)	0	Dietary Fiber (g)	0
Carbohydrate (g)	16	Sodium (mg)	80
Fat (g)	4	Cholesterol (mg)	0
Cal. from Fat (%)	37		

Orange and Walnut Green Salad

I always mix a variety of lettuce or mesclun for this fabulous salad. Simple yet elegant!

¼ cup orange juice
1 tablespoon olive oil
¼ teaspoon salt
Dash of hot sauce
6-8 cups assorted lettuce leaves

2 navel oranges, peeled and sectioned
½ red onion, thinly sliced
¼ cup chopped walnuts, toasted

Prepare the dressing in a small bowl by whisking the orange juice, oil, salt, and hot sauce. In a large salad bowl, combine lettuce, oranges, onion, and walnuts. Drizzle with the dressing, tossing to coat. Serve at once.

Makes 6 to 8 servings

Food Facts:
Onions, along with garlic, leeks, and chives, contain organosulfur compounds, which are cancer protective substances.

NUTRITIONAL INFORMATION PER SERVING

Calories	70	Saturated Fat (g)	0
Protein (g)	2	Dietary Fiber (g)	2
Carbohydrate (g)	8	Sodium (mg)	15
Fat (g)	4	Cholesterol (mg)	0
Cal. from Fat (%)	48		

Spinach Salad

The sweet, tart dressing tossed with the fresh fruit makes this a popular salad. Use available seasonal fruit to prepare year round.

Salad

1 (16-ounce) package spinach, stemmed and washed
1 nectarine, coarsely chopped
1 cup seedless red grapes
½ cup thinly sliced red onion
½ cup sliced mushrooms
2 tablespoons pine nuts, toasted
Sweet Sour Dressing (recipe follows)

In a large bowl, combine all the ingredients except dressing. Toss with dressing just before serving.

Makes 6 servings

Note: To toast pine nuts, place in toaster oven and set toaster to light.

Sweet Sour Dressing

⅔ cup balsamic vinegar
½ teaspoon minced garlic
1 teaspoon dry mustard
¼ cup light brown sugar
2 tablespoons olive oil

Mix together all dressing ingredients with a fork or whisk.

Food Facts:
This dressing can be sprinkled on cold, leftover cooked vegetables!

Healthier Approach:
For extra crunch and Vitamin C, add a bit of thinly sliced jícama strips. (Once you try jícama, you'll want to serve it as an hors d'oeuvre with reduced-fat dip.)

NUTRITIONAL INFORMATION PER SERVING

Calories	160	Saturated Fat (g)	1
Protein (g)	4	Dietary Fiber (g)	3
Carbohydrate (g)	25	Sodium (mg)	72
Fat (g)	7	Cholesterol (mg)	0
Cal. from Fat (%)	34		

Super Tossed Salad

This delicious salad is a colorful blend of greens,
reds, and white; perfect for a festive dinner party.

1 head Romaine lettuce, torn into pieces

¼ head iceberg lettuce, torn into pieces

1 (8-ounce) can sliced water chestnuts, drained

1 red apple, cored and thinly sliced

1 small red or green bell pepper, seeded and cut into strips

½ cup sliced green onions

¼ cup raspberry wine vinegar

2 tablespoons red wine vinegar

1 tablespoon olive oil

2 tablespoons honey

1 tablespoon water

Place the lettuce in a large bowl. Add the water chestnuts, apple, and green pepper. In a small bowl combine the green onion, raspberry wine vinegar, red wine vinegar, olive oil, honey, and water, mixing well. Just before serving, pour over the lettuce mixture and toss.

Makes 8 servings

Food Facts:

The greener the lettuce, the more nutrition it contains. In this salad, the iceberg lettuce provides more texture than nutrients.

NUTRITIONAL INFORMATION PER SERVING			
Calories	70	Saturated Fat (g)	0
Protein (g)	2	Dietary Fiber (g)	2
Carbohydrate (g)	11	Sodium (mg)	9
Fat (g)	3	Cholesterol (mg)	0
Cal. from Fat (%)	36		

Oven Fried Chicken

Eyebrows will raise when you put a plate of crispy fried chicken on the table. But thanks to the oven-bake method, you can indulge your cravings. Any part of the chicken, skin removed, can be used in this recipe.

1 cup buttermilk	2 cups Italian bread crumbs
Salt and pepper to taste	¼ cup grated Parmesan cheese
½ teaspoon minced garlic	2 tablespoons margarine or
2 pounds boneless skinless chicken breasts (approximately 6)	butter, melted

Combine the buttermilk, salt, pepper, and garlic. Pour over the chicken, turning to coat. Marinate, covered, 2 hours, or overnight in the refrigerator. Drain the chicken. In a small bowl, combine the bread crumbs and Parmesan cheese. Coat the chicken with this mixture and place on a baking sheet coated with nonstick cooking spray and chill for 30 minutes to 1 hour, time permitted. Preheat oven to 350 degrees. Drizzle the chicken with the margarine. Bake for 45 minutes to 1 hour, or until tender and golden brown.

Makes 6 to 8 servings

Food Facts:
Nonfat plain yogurt can be used in place of buttermilk.

NUTRITIONAL INFORMATION PER SERVING

Calories	284	Saturated Fat (g)	2
Protein (g)	32	Dietary Fiber (g)	1
Carbohydrate (g)	21	Sodium (mg)	435
Fat (g)	7	Cholesterol (mg)	69
Cal. from Fat (%)	23		

Parmesan Chicken Pasta

Another quick effortless dish that
includes ingredients your family will love.

2 tablespoons olive oil	1 teaspoon dried basil
2 pounds boneless skinless chicken breasts	1 cup chopped Roma tomatoes
	Salt and pepper to taste
1 tablespoon minced garlic	1 (16-ounce) package bow tie pasta
1 onion, chopped	
1 teaspoon dried thyme	⅓ cup grated Parmesan cheese
1 teaspoon dried oregano	

In a large skillet coated with nonstick cooking spray, heat the olive oil and cook the chicken for about 5 to 8 minutes or until lightly browned. Add the garlic and onions and continue cooking until the onion is tender. Add the thyme, oregano, basil, and tomatoes and continue cooking until the tomatoes are well heated, about 5 minutes. Season to taste with salt and pepper. Meanwhile, prepare pasta according to package directions omitting any oil and salt; drain. Toss the pasta with the chicken and add the cheese and mix until heated through.

Makes 8 servings

Healthier Approach:
Try serving over whole wheat pasta or brown rice.

NUTRITIONAL INFORMATION PER SERVING

Calories	401	Saturated Fat (g)	2
Protein (g)	36	Dietary Fiber (g)	2
Carbohydrate (g)	46	Sodium (mg)	157
Fat (g)	7	Cholesterol (mg)	69
Cal. from Fat (%)	16		

Chicken with Tomato Tarragon Sauce

My family enjoyed the simple, smooth,
yet seasoned sauce that I served over rice.

2 pounds boneless skinless chicken breasts	½ cup dry white wine or chicken broth
Salt and pepper to taste	1 (28-ounce) can tomato sauce
½ pound mushrooms, sliced	½ teaspoon dried tarragon
⅓ cup finely chopped green onions (scallions)	½ teaspoon dried thyme
	⅓ cup feta cheese, optional

Season chicken with salt and pepper to taste. In a large skillet coated with nonstick cooking spray, brown chicken pieces about 5 minutes per side. Season to taste. Add mushrooms and green onions and cook over medium heat, 3 minutes. Add wine and cook about 2 minutes, stirring to scrape browned bits from bottom of skillet. Stir in tomato sauce, tarragon, and thyme. Bring to a boil, reduce heat, cover and cook on medium-low heat for 15 to 20 minutes or until chicken is tender. If desired, sprinkle with feta and serve.

Makes 6 to 8 servings

Food Facts:

Tomato products offer lycopene, a substance currently being studied for its health protective qualities.

NUTRITIONAL INFORMATION PER SERVING

Calories	165	Saturated Fat (g)	0
Protein (g)	29	Dietary Fiber (g)	2
Carbohydrate (g)	9	Sodium (mg)	686
Fat (g)	2	Cholesterol (mg)	66
Cal. from Fat (%)	9		

Chicken Piccata

This recipe continually gets rave reviews in my house. Simple elegance.

½ cup all-purpose flour
Salt and pepper to taste
1 teaspoon dried oregano
2 pounds boneless skinless chicken breasts
3 tablespoons olive oil

2 cups canned fat-free chicken broth
1 teaspoon minced garlic
¼ cup lemon juice
2 tablespoons chopped parsley

In a small bowl, combine flour, salt, pepper, and oregano. Coat each chicken piece with mixture; set aside. In a skillet coated with nonstick cooking spray, heat oil and cook chicken breasts on each side until golden brown over medium-high heat. Remove chicken from pan as needed to brown all pieces. Add chicken broth, garlic, and lemon juice to pan, scraping sides of pan. Return chicken to pan, bring to a boil, reduce heat, cover and simmer for 10 to 15 minutes or until chicken is done. Sprinkle with parsley and serve.

Makes 6 to 8 servings

Healthier Approach:
Serve with a fresh steamed vegetable and seasoned brown rice.

NUTRITIONAL INFORMATION PER SERVING

Calories	209	Saturated Fat (g)	1
Protein (g)	29	Dietary Fiber (g)	0
Carbohydrate (g)	7	Sodium (mg)	117
Fat (g)	7	Cholesterol (mg)	66
Cal. from Fat (%)	29		

Basil Chicken

When I have run out of time in the day and need
something quick and special, I prepare this recipe. My
teenage son and his friends especially enjoy this dish.

½	cup all-purpose flour	1	tablespoon dried basil
	Salt and pepper to taste	1	(14½-ounce) can fat-free
2	pounds boneless, skinless		chicken broth
	chicken breasts, cut in strips	3	tablespoons lemon juice
1	teaspoon minced garlic		

In a bag or on a plate combine the flour with the salt and pepper. Coat the chicken with flour mixture very well and place in a large skillet coated with nonstick cooking spray. Cook the chicken for about 6 to 8 minutes or until browned. Add the garlic, basil, chicken broth, and lemon juice, stirring until chicken is well covered with the sauce. Bring to a boil, reduce heat, cover, and cook for 15 to 20 minutes or until the chicken is tender.

Makes 6 to 8 servings

Food Facts:

If using fresh basil in this recipe, use twice the amount of dried. The
dried herb is more flavor concentrated.

NUTRITIONAL INFORMATION PER SERVING

Calories	162	Saturated Fat (g)	0
Protein (g)	28	Dietary Fiber (g)	0
Carbohydrate (g)	7	Sodium (mg)	110
Fat (g)	1	Cholesterol (mg)	66
Cal. from Fat (%)	9		

Chicken Elegante

This heavenly sauce with artichokes and mushrooms
will certainly impress your guests. Make earlier and reheat.

2 pounds boneless skinless chicken breasts	1 cup canned fat-free chicken broth
Salt and pepper to taste	1 cup skim milk
2 tablespoons margarine, divided	½ teaspoon dried tarragon leaves
½ pound fresh mushrooms, sliced	1 (14-ounce) can quartered
1 tablespoon all-purpose flour	artichoke hearts, drained
1 (10¾-ounce) can low-fat cream of chicken soup	1 bunch green onions (scallions) chopped

Preheat oven to 350 degrees. Season the chicken with salt and pepper. In a large skillet coated with nonstick cooking spray, heat 1 tablespoon margarine until melted over a medium-high heat. Add the chicken and cook until brown on all sides, about 5 minutes. Remove the chicken and place in an oblong baking pan. In the same skillet, melt the remaining 1 tablespoon margarine and sauté the mushrooms until tender, about 5 minutes. Stir in the flour, soup, broth, milk, and tarragon. Season to taste. Bring to a boil, reduce the heat and cook, stirring, about 5 minutes. Pour the sauce over the chicken and bake, uncovered, for 50 minutes. Remove the chicken from the oven and top with the artichoke hearts and green onions. Return to the oven and continue baking for 15 minutes longer or until the chicken is done.

Makes 6 to 8 servings

Food Facts:
Artichokes contain a phytochemical called silymarin, which is believed to decrease the risk of skin cancer.

NUTRITIONAL INFORMATION PER SERVING

Calories	225	Saturated Fat (g)	1
Protein (g)	31	Dietary Fiber (g)	1
Carbohydrate (g)	11	Sodium (mg)	577
Fat (g)	5	Cholesterol (mg)	69
Cal. from Fat (%)	22		

Chicken and Broccoli

Broccoli seems to be a favorite veggie in my house.
Here's an easy way to prepare a complete dinner.

4	cups broccoli florets	1	(10¾-ounce) can low-fat	
1	red bell pepper, seeded and		cream of broccoli soup	
	cut into ¾-inch squares	½	cup water	
1	onion, chopped	1	teaspoon dried basil	
1	pound boneless skinless	½	cup shredded reduced-fat	
	chicken breasts, cut into		Cheddar cheese	
	strips	1	(8-ounce) package fettuccine	

In a large skillet coated with nonstick cooking spray, stir-fry the broccoli, red pepper, and onion until crisp-tender, about 4 minutes. Remove the vegetables from the skillet. Coat the pan again with nonstick cooking spray and add the chicken. Stir-fry until no longer pink, about 4 minutes. Add the cream of broccoli soup, water, and basil to the skillet. Mix well. Stir in the pepper mixture. Bring to a boil; reduce heat, and cook for 10 minutes. Add the cheese, stirring until the cheese is melted. Meanwhile, prepare the fettuccine according to the package directions, omitting any salt and oil. Drain and serve with the chicken and sauce.

Makes 4 servings

Food Facts:
Broccoli offers a substance called sulforaphane that helps to decrease cancer risk. Include it in your repertoire of vegetables eaten regularly!

NUTRITIONAL INFORMATION PER SERVING

Calories	387	Saturated Fat (g)	2
Protein (g)	39	Dietary Fiber (g)	5
Carbohydrate (g)	46	Sodium (mg)	717
Fat (g)	6	Cholesterol (mg)	72
Cal. from Fat (%)	13		

Chicken Rice Medley

The Southwestern seasoning, yellow rice, and colorful veggies make this dish eye and palate pleasing.

1	cup rice	2	tablespoons olive oil
1	(5-ounce) package saffron yellow long grain rice	1	cup canned fat-free chicken broth
2	tablespoons chili powder	1	(10-ounce) package frozen corn, thawed
1	tablespoon ground cumin	1	(15-ounce) can black beans, drained and rinsed
1	tablespoon paprika		
1	teaspoon garlic powder	¼	cup sliced green onions (scallions)
¼	teaspoon black pepper		
2	pounds boneless skinless chicken breasts, cut into strips		

Cook rice and saffron rice according to package directions. Combine chili powder, cumin, paprika, garlic powder, and pepper in a small bowl. Coat chicken strips with this mixture. In a large skillet, cook chicken in olive oil 8 to 10 minutes or until chicken is cooked. Add broth, cooked rice and saffron rice, corn, and black beans to chicken and cook 5 more minutes or until heated. Sprinkle with green onions and serve.

Makes 6 to 8 servings

Healthier Approach:
Add additional beans and corn, use less chicken.

NUTRITIONAL INFORMATION PER SERVING

Calories	381	Saturated Fat (g)	1
Protein (g)	34	Dietary Fiber (g)	5
Carbohydrate (g)	48	Sodium (mg)	562
Fat (g)	6	Cholesterol (mg)	66
Cal. from Fat (%)	14		

Chicken and Wild Rice Casserole

This one meal dish has a fancy touch with the
mushrooms, artichokes, and sherry. The recipe includes
several steps, but all in the same pan.

2 (6-ounce) packages long grain and wild rice mix	½ pound mushrooms, sliced
1 teaspoon paprika	¼ cup all-purpose flour
¼ teaspoon black pepper	½ teaspoon dried rosemary
2 pounds boneless skinless chicken breast halves	1 (16-ounce) can fat-free chicken broth
1 (14½-ounce) can artichoke hearts, drained and cut in half	½ cup dry sherry, optional

Preheat oven to 375 degrees. Cook the wild rice according to package directions, omitting any salt and oil. Spoon the cooked wild rice into a 2-quart oblong baking dish; set aside. Sprinkle paprika and pepper over the chicken; set aside. Coat a large skillet with nonstick cooking spray. Cook chicken over medium-high heat until lightly browned, about 5 minutes. Arrange the chicken on top of the rice. Top with the artichoke hearts, set aside. Add the mushrooms to the same skillet and sauté over a medium heat until tender, about 5 minutes. In a small bowl, combine the flour with the rosemary and gradually add the chicken broth and sherry, if using. Add this mixture to the skillet; cook for 3 minutes stirring constantly, or until thickened and bubbly. Spoon over the chicken. Bake, covered, for 45 minutes to 1 hour, until chicken is done.

Makes 8 servings

Healthier Approach:
Consider omitting the spice packet from the rice mixes and season to taste to lower sodium.

NUTRITIONAL INFORMATION PER SERVING

Calories	320	Saturated Fat (g)	0
Protein (g)	34	Dietary Fiber (g)	2
Carbohydrate (g)	41	Sodium (mg)	989
Fat (g)	2	Cholesterol (mg)	66
Cal. from Fat (%)	6		

Great Greek Chicken

When serving this dish, the sauce will be the talk of the table.
If you're not a feta fan, leave it out. Great served over orzo pasta.

2 pounds boneless skinless chicken breasts, cut into strips
1 green bell pepper, seeded and chopped
1 cup chopped green onions (scallions)

1 tablespoon dried basil
½ teaspoon dried oregano
½ teaspoon dried thyme
1 (28-ounce) can diced tomatoes with juice
1 teaspoon light brown sugar
½ cup crumbled feta cheese

In a large nonstick skillet coated with nonstick cooking spray, sauté the chicken and green pepper, over medium heat, about 5 to 7 minutes or until peppers are softened. Stir in green onions, basil, oregano, thyme, tomatoes, and sugar. Simmer about 15 minutes until the chicken is tender and the sauce thickens slightly. Before serving, stir in the cheese and serve chicken and sauce over pasta.

Makes 6 to 8 servings

NUTRITIONAL INFORMATION PER SERVING

Calories	203	Saturated Fat (g)	3
Protein (g)	30	Dietary Fiber (g)	1
Carbohydrate (g)	7	Sodium (mg)	455
Fat (g)	5	Cholesterol (mg)	82
Cal. from Fat (%)	25		

Chicken with Black Bean Sauce

This is so easy - you open a few cans and stir, then bake the whole dish in the oven. This knock your socks off dish is great served over rice and can also be served with condiments such as sliced green onions (scallions), salsa, and shredded reduced-fat Cheddar cheese.

½ cup chopped onion
½ teaspoon minced garlic
1 (16-ounce) can black beans, rinsed and drained
1 (16-ounce) can diced tomatoes, with their juice
1 (4-ounce) can chopped green chiles, drained

1 tablespoon chili powder
1 tablespoon ground cumin
1 teaspoon ground coriander
2 pounds boneless skinless chicken breasts
Salt and pepper to taste

Preheat oven to 350 degrees. In a pot coated with nonstick cooking spray, sauté the onion and garlic over medium heat until tender, about 5 minutes. Stir in the black beans, tomatoes with juice, green chiles, chili powder, cumin, and coriander. Bring to a boil; reduce the heat and simmer 5 minutes. In a 2-quart oblong ovenproof pan, season the chicken breasts with salt and pepper. Pour the black bean sauce over the chicken. Bake, covered with foil, for 45 minutes to 1 hour, until the chicken is cooked through.

Makes 6 to 8 servings

Food Facts:
Enjoy leftovers wrapped in a whole wheat tortilla.

NUTRITIONAL INFORMATION PER SERVING

Calories	187	Saturated Fat (g)	0
Protein (g)	31	Dietary Fiber (g)	4
Carbohydrate (g)	11	Sodium (mg)	579
Fat (g)	2	Cholesterol (mg)	66
Cal. from Fat (%)	9		

Salsa Chicken

Simple yet tasty. With this wonderfully spicy sauce, rice is the perfect accompaniment.

2½ pounds boneless skinless
    chicken breasts
Black pepper to taste
1 cup mild salsa
1 tablespoon minced garlic
1 (10-ounce) can diced
    tomatoes and green chiles

1 (11-ounce) can shoe peg corn,
    drained
1½ cups shredded reduced-fat
    Monterey Jack cheese
½ cup sliced green onions
    (scallions)

Preheat oven to 350 degrees. Cut the chicken breasts into strips. Place in a 2-quart casserole dish and sprinkle with pepper. Spoon the salsa, garlic, tomatoes and chiles, and corn over the chicken. Mix well. Cover and bake for 1 hour. Uncover and sprinkle with cheese and green onions. Continue cooking for 5 minutes or until the cheese is melted.

Makes 8 to 10 servings

Food Facts:

Salsa is the most popular condiment - it's no longer ketchup! Purchase a jar or toss a few ripe tomatoes, onions, and jalapeños in the food processor and blend to desired consistency.

NUTRITIONAL INFORMATION PER SERVING

Calories	214	Saturated Fat (g)	2
Protein (g)	33	Dietary Fiber (g)	1
Carbohydrate (g)	9	Sodium (mg)	474
Fat (g)	5	Cholesterol (mg)	75
Cal. from Fat (%)	21		

Stuffed Chicken Breasts with Enchilada Sauce

The kids really enjoy this flavorful dish. Leave out the green chiles or reduce the amount to accommodate your family.

2 pounds boneless skinless chicken breasts	1 teaspoon ground cumin
1 (4-ounce) can green chiles, drained	Salt and pepper to taste
2 tablespoons minced garlic	1 cup fat-free sour cream
4 ounces reduced-fat Monterey Jack cheese, cut into slices	1 (14-ounce) can enchilada sauce
1½ cups bread crumbs	1 cup corn (thawed if using frozen)
1 tablespoon chili powder	Sliced green onions (scallions)

Spread each piece of chicken with the green chiles and garlic. Top with cheese slice and roll up. Secure with toothpick if needed. Combine bread crumbs, chili powder, cumin, salt, and pepper. Dip each chicken roll in sour cream and roll in crumb mixture. Place breasts, seam side down, in baking dish. Chill for at least 1 hour. Preheat oven to 400 degrees. Mix enchilada sauce with corn and pour enchilada sauce over chicken. Cook for 45 minutes or until chicken is done. Sprinkle with green onions before serving.

Makes 6 to 8 servings

NUTRITIONAL INFORMATION PER SERVING

Calories	328	Saturated Fat (g)	2
Protein (g)	36	Dietary Fiber (g)	3
Carbohydrate (g)	31	Sodium (mg)	964
Fat (g)	5	Cholesterol (mg)	78
Cal. from Fat (%)	15		

Maple Dijon Glazed Turkey Breast

*My family enjoys this tasty turkey breast year round
and leftovers make great sandwiches.*

1 (5 to 6-pound) turkey breast	½ cup canned fat-free chicken
1 small orange, cut in half	broth
1 small onion, cut in half	¼ cup Dijon mustard
½ cup pure maple syrup	4 garlic cloves, cut in slivers
	Salt and pepper to taste

Preheat oven to 325 degrees. Wash and pat dry turkey and put in roasting pan. Stuff the orange and onion in the turkey cavity. In a small bowl, mix together the maple syrup, chicken broth, and mustard; set aside. With a knife, make slits throughout the turkey and stuff with garlic. Pour sauce all over turkey. Season to taste with salt and pepper. Bake for 2 to 2½ hours or until thermometer registers 170 degrees. Baste with glaze every 30 minutes. Cover the breast loosely with foil if it gets too brown.

Makes 16 servings

Food Facts:
Using Dijon mustard in recipes helps to keep the salt content low, but with great flavor.

Healthier Approach:
Freeze leftovers in individual portion sizes and defrost when a quick meal (turkey salad or sandwich) is needed.

NUTRITIONAL INFORMATION PER SERVING

Calories	189	Saturated Fat (g)	0
Protein (g)	35	Dietary Fiber (g)	1
Carbohydrate (g)	7	Sodium (mg)	170
Fat (g)	1	Cholesterol (mg)	88
Cal. from Fat (%)	6		

Italian Shrimp and Pasta

You definitely need a loaf of French bread to dip into the sauce.
This is a variation of barbecued shrimp, with peeled shrimp
so it is not so messy to eat. The sauce is one of the best,
and, in this case, is the "dish" itself!

2 tablespoons margarine or butter
½ cup fat-fee Italian dressing
1 tablespoon minced garlic
¼ cup Worcestershire sauce
1 teaspoon dried oregano
1 teaspoon dried rosemary
1 teaspoon dried thyme
¼ cup lemon juice
1 teaspoon paprika
2 pounds medium to large shrimp, peeled
1 cup coarsely chopped tomatoes
1 (16-ounce) package angel hair pasta
½ cup chopped green onions, optional

In a large skillet, melt the margarine and add the Italian dressing, garlic, Worcestershire sauce, oregano, rosemary, thyme, lemon juice, and paprika. Bring to a boil over medium heat and add the shrimp and tomatoes, cooking until the shrimp are done, about 7 minutes. Meanwhile, prepare the pasta according to the package directions, omitting any salt and oil. Drain and toss the shrimp and sauce with the pasta. Sprinkle with green onions, if desired.

Makes 8 servings

Food Facts:
Shrimp contain almost no saturated fat.

NUTRITIONAL INFORMATION PER SERVING

Calories	328	Saturated Fat (g)	1
Protein (g)	31	Dietary Fiber (g)	1
Carbohydrate (g)	37	Sodium (mg)	629
Fat (g)	6	Cholesterol (mg)	172
Cal. from Fat (%)	16		

Shrimp Stir-Fry with Toasted Pecans

This is a great last minute dish that has a
super flavor with the touch of pecans. Serve over rice.

4	cups broccoli florets	1	pound medium shrimp, peeled
⅔	cup canned fat-free chicken broth	1	(6-ounce) package frozen snow pea pods, thawed
1	tablespoon cornstarch	1	tablespoon chopped pecans,
1	teaspoon ground ginger		toasted
1	tablespoon minced garlic	⅓	cup sliced green onions
1	large red or green bell pepper, seeded and chopped		(scallions)

In a microwave safe dish, cook the broccoli, covered with ½ cup water for 6 to 8 minutes or until crisp-tender. Drain; set aside. In a small bowl combine the chicken broth, cornstarch, and ginger until mixed. Set aside. In a large skillet coated with nonstick cooking spray, sauté the garlic and red pepper for a few minutes. Add the shrimp and broth mixture and continue stirring and cooking until the shrimp are done and the sauce thickens. Add the broccoli, pea pods, pecans, and green onions. Cook 1 minute longer or until well heated.

Makes 4 servings

NUTRITIONAL INFORMATION PER SERVING

Calories	198	Saturated Fat (g)	1
Protein (g)	28	Dietary Fiber (g)	3
Carbohydrate (g)	13	Sodium (mg)	219
Fat (g)	3	Cholesterol (mg)	172
Cal. from Fat (%)	16		

Shrimp and Spinach Pasta Toss

A super tasting, colorful, and easy dish to throw together.

2 tablespoons olive oil	2 cups fresh spinach leaves,
2 pounds shrimp, peeled and deveined	washed and stemmed
¼ cup chopped green onions (scallions), chopped	1 (16-ounce) package penne pasta
Salt and pepper to taste	1 cup finely chopped tomatoes
	3 tablespoons pine nuts, toasted

In a large skillet, heat olive oil until hot. Add shrimp and green onions. Sauté until shrimp are pink, about 5 minutes. Salt and pepper to taste. Add spinach leaves and cook only until spinach is wilted. Cook pasta according to package directions, omitting any oil and salt; drain. Pour shrimp mixture over the pasta. Toss with tomatoes and pine nuts.

Makes 8 servings

Food Facts:

A delicious way to get your greens! Try kale, too, instead of spinach. Shrimp are high in omega 3: a polyunsaturated fatty acid found primarily in certain seafood.

NUTRITIONAL INFORMATION PER SERVING

Calories	387	Saturated Fat (g)	1
Protein (g)	32	Dietary Fiber (g)	2
Carbohydrate (g)	46	Sodium (mg)	186
Fat (g)	8	Cholesterol (mg)	173
Cal. from Fat (%)	19		

Greek Shrimp Bake

This dish has more flavor than can be described.
We loved it over pasta or rice because the sauce was fabulous.

1   onion, chopped
2   tablespoons olive oil
1   (28-ounce) can diced or
    quartered tomatoes,
    undrained
½   cup chopped fresh parsley
1   tablespoon minced garlic
1   tablespoon dried oregano

Salt and pepper to taste
2   pounds medium shrimp,
    peeled
1   (10-ounce) package frozen
    peas, thawed and drained
½   cup crumbled feta cheese,
    optional

Preheat oven to 375 degrees. In a large skillet, over medium heat, sauté onion in olive oil until tender. Stir in tomatoes, parsley, garlic, oregano, salt, and pepper. Reduce heat to low, cover skillet and gently simmer mixture for 20 minutes, stirring occasionally. Remove sauce from stove; stir in shrimp and peas. Transfer mixture to a 2-quart baking dish. Sprinkle with feta cheese. Bake, uncovered, for 20 to 30 minutes or until shrimp are done.

Makes 6 to 8 servings

Food Facts:
Shrimp are low in calories and saturated fat and full of flavor.

NUTRITIONAL INFORMATION PER SERVING

Calories	208	Saturated Fat (g)	1
Protein (g)	26	Dietary Fiber (g)	3
Carbohydrate (g)	12	Sodium (mg)	371
Fat (g)	5	Cholesterol (mg)	172
Cal. from Fat (%)	24		

Shrimp Soft Tacos with Cranberry Salsa

*Outstanding! The shrimp, with the Southwest flavor,
make this a taco to remember. Serve with this delicious cranberry
salsa or commercially prepared salsa. Cranberry
salsa complements turkey or pork, also.*

1 green bell pepper, seeded and sliced
1 onion, sliced in thin rings and cut in half
1 teaspoon minced garlic
1½ pounds medium shrimp, peeled
1 teaspoon ground cumin
½ teaspoon chili powder
1 (10-ounce) can diced tomatoes and green chiles, drained
2 tablespoons chopped fresh cilantro, optional
10 (6 to 8-inch) flour tortillas, heated
1¼ cups shredded reduced-fat Monterey Jack cheese
Cranberry salsa (recipe follows)

In a large skillet coated with nonstick cooking spray, sauté the green pepper, onion, and garlic over medium-high heat for 2 minutes. Add the shrimp, cumin, and chili powder. Continue cooking for 5 minutes. Add the tomatoes and cilantro, if using. Cook for a few minutes longer or until the shrimp are done. On each flour tortilla, divide evenly the shrimp mixture and Monterey Jack cheese and fold over in half. If desired, heat in the microwave for 30 seconds or until the cheese is melted. Serve with the Cranberry Salsa.

Makes 10 shrimp tacos

Cranberry Salsa

2 cups chopped cranberries
2 cups chopped oranges
⅓ cup orange juice
⅓ cup chopped red onion
1 tablespoon sugar
⅓ cup chopped fresh cilantro
2 tablespoons diced green chiles

In a large bowl, mix together the cranberries, oranges, orange juice, onion, sugar, cilantro, and green chiles. Chill until ready to serve.

Makes about 5 cups

Food Facts:
Although shrimp is relatively high in cholesterol, its fat content (and saturated fat) is very low.

Soft Shrimp Tacos *continued*

Healthier Approach:
Use whole wheat tortillas or fat-free tortillas.

NUTRITIONAL INFORMATION PER SERVING

Calories	313	Saturated Fat (g)	3
Protein (g)	23	Dietary Fiber (g)	3
Carbohydrate (g)	40	Sodium (mg)	669
Fat (g)	7	Cholesterol (mg)	114
Cal. from Fat (%)	20		

Shrimp, Asparagus, and Brie Pasta

These ingredients are a little costly but definitely worth the buy! Perfect when asparagus are in season.

½   cup chopped onion
1   teaspoon minced garlic
1   bundle asparagus spears, trimmed and cut in 2-inch pieces
2   pounds medium shrimp, peeled
1   (16-ounce) package penne pasta
4   ounces Brie cheese
1   teaspoon dried oregano
½   cup sliced green onions (scallions)

In a nonstick skillet, sauté onion, garlic, and asparagus for 3 minutes. Add shrimp and continue cooking until shrimp are done, 5 to 7 minutes. Meanwhile cook pasta according to package directions omitting any oil and salt; drain and add to shrimp mixture. Add Brie, oregano, and green onions, stirring until Brie is melted.

Makes 6 to 8 servings

NUTRITIONAL INFORMATION PER SERVING

Calories	388	Saturated Fat (g)	3
Protein (g)	34	Dietary Fiber (g)	2
Carbohydrate (g)	46	Sodium (mg)	264
Fat (g)	7	Cholesterol (mg)	187
Cal. from Fat (%)	16		

Shrimp Enchiladas

Serve these creamy cheesy shrimp
enchiladas with your favorite salsa.

1 cup chopped onion
1 tablespoon chopped garlic
2 tablespoons all-purpose flour
1 teaspoon dried oregano
1 teaspoon dried basil
1 teaspoon dried thyme
Dash of cayenne pepper
3 tablespoons chopped cilantro
2 teaspoons ground cumin

1 sliced jalapeño pepper,
   optional
Salt and pepper to taste
1 cup evaporated skimmed milk
1 pound medium peeled shrimp,
   cooked
1¼ cups shredded reduced-fat
   Monterey Jack cheese, divided
8 (10-inch) flour or wheat
   tortillas, room temperature

Preheat oven to 350 degrees. In a skillet coated with nonstick cooking spray, sauté onion and garlic over medium heat for several minutes. Add flour and stir well; add oregano, basil, thyme, cayenne, cilantro, cumin, jalapeño, salt, and pepper and gradually add milk. Reduce heat and cook until very thick; remove from heat; cool slightly. Fold in shrimp and ¾ cup cheese. Place 2 tablespoons of the filling on each tortilla and roll up. Place rolled tortillas side by side in a 2-quart baking dish coated with nonstick cooking spray and top with remaining ½ cup cheese. Bake for 5 minutes or until cheese is melted and dish is well heated.

Makes 6 to 8 servings

Healthier Approach:
Use fat-free tortillas. Amount of cheese can be decreased, if desired.

NUTRITIONAL INFORMATION PER SERVING

Calories	389	Saturated Fat (g)	3
Protein (g)	26	Dietary Fiber (g)	3
Carbohydrate (g)	48	Sodium (mg)	577
Fat (g)	9	Cholesterol (mg)	97
Cal. from Fat (%)	22		

Scallops with Black Beans

*The scallops have a wonderful Southwestern flair
and would be great tossed with pasta.*

1½ pounds sea scallops
1½ teaspoons olive oil
1   teaspoon ground cumin,
    divided
½ teaspoon minced garlic
Dash of cayenne pepper

1   bunch green onions
    (scallions), chopped
1   (15-ounce) can black beans,
    drained and rinsed
1   teaspoon balsamic vinegar

Place scallops in a shallow dish. Combine olive oil, ½ teaspoon cumin, garlic, and cayenne; drizzle over scallops, and toss gently. Cover; marinate in refrigerator 30 minutes, stirring occasionally. Coat a large nonstick skillet with cooking spray; place over heat until hot. Add scallops, discarding marinade, and onion; cook over medium-high heat until scallops are done; opaque in color. Stir in black beans and remaining ½ teaspoon cumin; sauté until thoroughly heated. Remove from heat; stir in vinegar and serve.

Makes 6 servings

Food Facts:
Scallops are low in fat. Serve with seasoned bulgur and fresh tomato and pepper slices.

NUTRITIONAL INFORMATION PER SERVING

Calories	171	Saturated Fat (g)	0
Protein (g)	23	Dietary Fiber (g)	4
Carbohydrate (g)	13	Sodium (mg)	404
Fat (g)	3	Cholesterol (mg)	37
Cal. from Fat (%)	14		

Crab Cakes with Horseradish Caper Sauce

Make ahead and refrigerate until ready to prepare.
These make a great dinner.

Crab Cakes

1 pound lump crabmeat, picked for shells	1 large egg, beaten slightly
⅓ cup finely chopped green onions (scallions)	2 tablespoons Dijon mustard
¼ cup diced onions	1 tablespoon lemon juice
½ cup chopped green bell peppers	1 teaspoon Worcestershire sauce
1 teaspoon minced garlic	2 cups fresh bread crumbs, divided

In a bowl, mix together crabmeat, green onion, onion, green pepper, and garlic. In a separate small bowl, combine egg, mustard, lemon juice, and Worcestershire sauce. Add about ¼ cup bread crumbs to crab mixture and fold in egg mixture carefully. With your hand, form into eight patties and coat with remaining bread crumbs. Place on a baking sheet in refrigerator and chill for several hours or until needed. Heat a large nonstick skillet coated with nonstick cooking spray over medium heat. Cook the crab cakes about 4 minutes on each side, turning once, until golden brown. Serve with Horseradish Caper Sauce.

Makes 8 servings

Healthier Approach:
Serve with those summer-fresh steamed vegetables - green beans, zucchini, yellow squash, broccoli, and fresh sliced tomatoes.

Horseradish Caper Sauce

¼ cup light mayonnaise	1 tablespoon finely chopped onion
2 tablespoons prepared horseradish	1 teaspoon capers, drained
1 tablespoon lemon juice	

Stir all ingredients together and refrigerate.

Crab Cakes *continued*

MAIN DISHES

NUTRITIONAL INFORMATION PER SERVING

Calories	219	Saturated Fat (g)	1
Protein (g)	17	Dietary Fiber (g)	1
Carbohydrate (g)	24	Sodium (mg)	625
Fat (g)	6	Cholesterol (mg)	70
Cal. from Fat (%)	24		

Pan Smoked Salmon Southwestern Style

This simple method of indoor smoking gives you the incredible smoked flavor found in the restaurants without even having to use an outdoor grill. The Southwestern seasoning gives this dish a sensational flavor. The pan is lined with foil so clean up is a breeze.

4	(5-ounce) filets of salmon		Black pepper to taste
½	teaspoon ground cumin	1	tablespoon lemon juice
½	teaspoon chili powder		Mesquite smoked chips
1	teaspoon minced garlic		(about 2 cups)

Season the salmon with cumin, chili powder, garlic, and pepper to taste. Drizzle with lemon juice. Soak the chips in a bowl of water for 30 minutes. Line a large skillet with foil. Drain the chips and place in a pile in the middle of the pan. Place a rack (cooling rack or fish rack) coated with nonstick cooking spray over the chips. Place the seasoned salmon filets on the rack. Cover with foil. Heat the pan over a medium high heat until it begins smoking. Lower the heat and continue to smoke for 25 to 30 minutes or until done. Make sure the overhead vent is turned on. When done, remove the salmon and serve.

Makes 4 servings

Food Facts:
Enjoy those salmon dishes - they contain lots of omega-3 fatty acids, which are being studied for many protective health benefits.

NUTRITIONAL INFORMATION PER SERVING

Calories	263	Saturated Fat (g)	3
Protein (g)	28	Dietary Fiber (g)	0
Carbohydrate (g)	1	Sodium (mg)	84
Fat (g)	15	Cholesterol (mg)	84
Cal. from Fat (%)	54		

Simply Salmon Pasta

An elegant blend of ingredients and flavors.
This is a great method to prepare pan-seared salmon, also.

1 (8-ounce) package spinach tortellini	1 cup clam juice
1 (12-ounce) package bow tie pasta	⅔ cup evaporated skimmed milk
8 ounces salmon filets	1 cup sugar snap peas
Salt and pepper to taste	½ cup green onions (scallions)
¼ teaspoon sugar	1 teaspoon dried dill weed
	⅓ cup grated Parmesan cheese

In a large pot of boiling water, add the spinach tortellini and cook for about 10 minutes. To the same pot, add the bow tie pasta and continue cooking until pasta is done. Drain and set aside. Season the salmon with salt, pepper, and sugar. In a skillet coated with nonstick cooking spray, cook the salmon skin side down on medium-high heat. Turn to other side and cook until done. Remove skin and cut in chunks and set aside. In the same skillet, add clam juice and evaporated milk. Bring to a boil, reduce heat and simmer until liquid reduces, about 7 minutes. Add the peas and green onions cooking several minutes or until peas are crisp-tender. Add the cooked pasta, dill, and cheese, tossing carefully. Carefully toss in the salmon.

Makes 6 to 8 servings

Healthier Approach:
Use reduced-sodium broth instead of clam juice to help control sodium.

NUTRITIONAL INFORMATION PER SERVING

Calories	318	Saturated Fat (g)	2
Protein (g)	18	Dietary Fiber (g)	2
Carbohydrate (g)	43	Sodium (mg)	1583
Fat (g)	8	Cholesterol (mg)	59
Cal. from Fat (%)	22		

Glazed Salmon with Cantaloupe Salsa

A superb method to prepare salmon with a syrupy sauce. When cantaloupe is in season, try this delicious salsa which perfectly complements the salmon.

1   tablespoon margarine, melted
½   cup light brown sugar
3   tablespoons reduced-sodium soy sauce
2   tablespoons lemon juice

2   tablespoons white wine, optional
2   pounds salmon filets
Cantaloupe Salsa (recipe follows)

In a shallow glass dish, mix together margarine, brown sugar, soy sauce, lemon juice, and wine. Add salmon and cover with marinade. Refrigerate for 30 minutes to several hours. Place salmon and marinade on foil-lined pan and bake at 400 degrees for 15 minutes or until salmon is done, basting with sauce. Salmon may be grilled, also. Spoon Cantaloupe Salsa alongside the salmon.

Makes 6 servings

Cantaloupe Salsa

¾   cup coarsely chopped cantaloupe
¼   cup chopped red onion
2   tablespoons chopped fresh cilantro
1   cup cherry tomatoes, halved

2   tablespoons olive oil
1   tablespoon lemon juice
1   teaspoon minced and seeded jalapeño pepper
Salt and pepper to taste

Mix the cantaloupe, onion, cilantro, tomatoes, olive oil, lemon juice, and jalapeño in a small bowl. Season with salt and pepper. Let stand for 15 minutes.

Makes 2 cups

Food Facts:
Salmon is a "fatty" fish, providing a good supply of health-protective omega-3 fatty acids.

NUTRITIONAL INFORMATION PER SERVING

Calories	300	Saturated Fat (g)	3
Protein (g)	23	Dietary Fiber (g)	0
Carbohydrate (g)	16	Sodium (mg)	433
Fat (g)	16	Cholesterol (mg)	67
Cal. from Fat (%)	47		

Marinated Tuna with Pineapple Salsa

A perfect entrée for entertaining, the tuna is cooked on the grill just before serving; the marinade may be made well ahead of time.

½ cup seasoned rice vinegar	¼ teaspoon crushed red pepper flakes
½ cup finely chopped green onions (scallions)	6 Ahi tuna steaks (about 1-inch thick)
1 tablespoon Dijon mustard	Pineapple Salsa (recipe follows)

In a shallow non-aluminum bowl, combine the vinegar, onions, mustard, and pepper. Coat the tuna with the marinade and marinate for several hours, refrigerated, turning occasionally. Light a fire in a charcoal grill or preheat the broiler. Remove the tuna from the refrigerator 30 minutes before cooking. Broil or grill the tuna 4 to 6 inches from the broiler or very hot coals, 4 to 5 minutes per side for rare to medium rare doneness.

Makes 6 servings

Pineapple Salsa

This sweet spicy salsa is great with grilled dishes or chips.

1 (16-ounce) can pineapple, drained	1 tablespoon seasoned rice vinegar
½ cup diced red bell pepper	¼ cup finely chopped green onions (scallions)
½ cup diced green bell pepper	⅛ teaspoon crushed red pepper flakes
½ cup finely chopped red onion	Salt and pepper to taste
3 tablespoons minced fresh cilantro	

In a large non-aluminum bowl, combine all the ingredients and adjust seasoning. Refrigerate until ready to serve.

Makes about 3 cups

Food Facts:
Fruit "salsas" are now in vogue...a great way to get a wide variety of phytochemicals for better health. Tuna is high in protein and low in fat.

NUTRITIONAL INFORMATION PER SERVING

Calories	214	Saturated Fat (g)	1
Protein (g)	33	Dietary Fiber (g)	2
Carbohydrate (g)	16	Sodium (mg)	121
Fat (g)	2	Cholesterol (mg)	68
Cal. from Fat (%)	8		

Spicy Topped Trout

This quickly made topping will turn a fish filet into a gourmet delight. My daughter's friend said it didn't even taste like fish it was so good.

2   pounds trout filets
Salt and pepper to taste
3   tablespoons balsamic vinegar
¼   cup light mayonnaise
1   tablespoon lemon juice
1   teaspoon Worcestershire sauce

1   teaspoon minced garlic
½   teaspoon sugar
1   teaspoon Dijon mustard
Dash of cayenne pepper
Paprika

Preheat oven to 500 degrees. Rinse the trout, pat dry, and lay in an oblong pan. Season to taste with salt and pepper and drizzle with the balsamic vinegar. In a small bowl, mix together the mayonnaise, lemon juice, Worcestershire sauce, garlic, sugar, Dijon mustard, and cayenne. Spread the mayonnaise mixture over the filets. Let sit to marinate for about 20 minutes. Sprinkle with paprika. Bake the fish for 10 to 15 minutes or until the fish flakes with a fork.

Makes 6 to 8 servings

Healthier Approach:
Serve with fresh steamed vegetables and your favorite grains.

NUTRITIONAL INFORMATION PER SERVING

Calories	189	Saturated Fat (g)	2
Protein (g)	24	Dietary Fiber (g)	0
Carbohydrate (g)	2	Sodium (mg)	119
Fat (g)	9	Cholesterol (mg)	67
Cal. from Fat (%)	43		

Trout Almandine

If you're a fried fish person, you will enjoy this crunchy coating.

½ cup buttermilk
⅓ cup finely chopped almonds
1 cup Italian bread crumbs

2 pounds trout filets
¼ cup lemon juice

Pour the buttermilk into a shallow bowl. Mix together the almonds and bread crumbs on a plate. Dip the trout filets into the buttermilk and then roll in the bread crumb mixture coating evenly, set aside. Coat a large nonstick skillet with nonstick cooking spray and heat to a medium heat. Add the filets and cook for about 4 minutes on each side or until lightly browned. Remove fish from skillet and keep warm. After all fish has been sautéed, add the lemon juice scraping the sides of the pan. Drizzle the lemon juice over the fish.

Makes 8 servings

Food Facts:
Although the name implies high in calories, buttermilk is actually made from skim or low-fat milk.

NUTRITIONAL INFORMATION PER SERVING

Calories	251	Saturated Fat (g)	2
Protein (g)	27	Dietary Fiber (g)	1
Carbohydrate (g)	12	Sodium (mg)	271
Fat (g)	10	Cholesterol (mg)	67
Cal. from Fat (%)	36		

Mediterranean Red Snapper

The feta baked with the red sauce and green beans form a wonderful sauce that would also be great with any choice of fish or chicken.

1   onion, chopped
1   (14½-ounce) can diced
      tomatoes, with their juice
1   (8-ounce) can tomato sauce
½   teaspoon sugar
1   tablespoon dried oregano

2   pounds red snapper filets, cut
      into 1-inch pieces
1   (16-ounce) package frozen cut
      green beans, partially thawed
1   cup crumbled feta cheese
Salt and pepper to taste

Preheat the oven to 350 degrees. In a medium skillet coated with nonstick cooking spray, sauté the onion until tender, about 3 to 4 minutes. Stir in the tomatoes, tomato sauce, sugar, and oregano. Bring to a boil, reduce the heat and simmer uncovered, for 15 minutes. Arrange the fish in a 2-quart oblong baking dish coated with nonstick cooking spray. Top with the green beans. Pour the sauce evenly over the fish and sprinkle with the cheese. Bake for 25 to 30 minutes or until the fish flakes easily. Salt and pepper to taste.

Makes 8 servings

Food Facts:
This sauce can be used to accompany other fish filets, as well as chicken, poached, roasted, or grilled.

NUTRITIONAL INFORMATION PER SERVING

Calories	198	Saturated Fat (g)	3
Protein (g)	27	Dietary Fiber (g)	2
Carbohydrate (g)	8	Sodium (mg)	606
Fat (g)	6	Cholesterol (mg)	59
Cal. from Fat (%)	26		

Super Snapper

*You can actually use this same simply delicious recipe for
shrimp or chicken, just bake longer until the chicken is cooked.*

1	pound snapper filets	1	tablespoon dried basil
⅓	cup balsamic vinegar	2	tablespoons grated Parmesan
2	tablespoons lemon juice		cheese
⅓	cup Italian bread crumbs		

Preheat the oven to 400 degrees. Lay the snapper filets on a baking sheet
lined with foil. Sprinkle with the balsamic vinegar and lemon juice. In a small
dish, combine the bread crumbs, basil, and Parmesan cheese. Sprinkle over
the fish. Bake for 15 minutes or until the fish is done.

Makes 4 servings

Food Facts:

*Serve with a chewy grain dish, such as brown rice or quinoa mixed
with your favorite herbs or spices, a bit of olive oil, and steamed chopped
veggies.*

NUTRITIONAL INFORMATION PER SERVING

Calories	179	Saturated Fat (g)	1
Protein (g)	26	Dietary Fiber (g)	0
Carbohydrate (g)	10	Sodium (mg)	278
Fat (g)	3	Cholesterol (mg)	44
Cal. from Fat (%)	16		

Stuffed Flounder Florentine

An easy way to enjoy stuffed fish. The spinach stuffing made with fresh spinach, and a touch of cheese combined with dill seasoned flounder proves to be an attractive presentation with a flavor to match.

1 onion, chopped
½ pound mushrooms, sliced
1 teaspoon minced garlic
1 (10-ounce) package fresh
   spinach, washed and
   stemmed
¼ cup Italian bread crumbs

⅓ cup shredded reduced-fat
   Cheddar cheese
   Salt and pepper to taste
2 pounds flounder filets
1 tablespoon dried dill weed
½ cup white wine, chicken broth,
   or clam juice
   Paprika

Preheat oven to 350 degrees. In a skillet coated with nonstick cooking spray, sauté the onion, mushrooms, and garlic until tender. Gradually add the spinach, stirring until just wilted. Add the bread crumbs and cheese, stirring until melted. Season to taste. Season the flounder with the dill, salt, and pepper. Divide the stuffing among the flounder filets and roll the fish up around the stuffing. Secure rolls with a toothpick. Lay each roll in an oblong glass baking dish coated with nonstick cooking spray. Pour the wine in the dish. Sprinkle the rolls with paprika. Bake for 20 to 25 minutes or until the fish flakes with a fork.

Makes 6 servings

Food Facts:
Spinach is a great way to "sneak in" vegetables. Try this with kale for a change of pace.

NUTRITIONAL INFORMATION PER SERVING

Calories	148	Saturated Fat (g)	1
Protein (g)	25	Dietary Fiber (g)	1
Carbohydrate (g)	7	Sodium (mg)	266
Fat (g)	2	Cholesterol (mg)	55
Cal. from Fat (%)	14		

Fish with Horseradish Mustard Sauce

*The horseradish and dry mustard give this fish a
bite, and the Parmesan cheese and dill round out the flavor.
A fabulous combination that even my kids, the
toughest judges, said was a winner!*

2   pounds fish filets (trout,
    snapper, orange roughy, or
    your favorite)
Salt and pepper to taste
½   cup plain nonfat yogurt
1   teaspoon cornstarch

1   tablespoon prepared
    horseradish
1   tablespoon dry mustard
¼   cup grated Parmesan cheese
2   tablespoons lemon juice
1   teaspoon dried dill weed
1   tablespoon capers, drained

Preheat the oven to 350 degrees. Season the filets with salt and pepper. In a small bowl, combine the yogurt, cornstarch, horseradish, dry mustard, Parmesan cheese, lemon juice, dill, and capers. Dip each filet in the sauce and lay in a baking dish coated with nonstick cooking spray. If extra sauce, spread over fish. Bake for 15 to 20 minutes, or until the fish flakes with a fork.

Makes 6 to 8 servings

Food Facts:
This mixture can be used on baked chicken, also.

NUTRITIONAL INFORMATION PER SERVING

Calories	102	Saturated Fat (g)	1
Protein (g)	19	Dietary Fiber (g)	0
Carbohydrate (g)	2	Sodium (mg)	176
Fat (g)	2	Cholesterol (mg)	25
Cal. from Fat (%)	16		

Stuffed Tenderloin

Make this incredible meat ahead and refrigerate
until ready to cook for an outstanding meal!

1 (5 to 6-pound) beef tenderloin
1 onion, chopped
1 tablespoon minced garlic
1 (10-ounce) bag fresh spinach, rinsed, stemmed and chopped
⅓ cup seasoned bread crumbs

⅓ cup grated Parmesan cheese
Salt and pepper to taste
Garlic powder to taste
¼ cup Worcestershire sauce
1 beef bouillon cube
1½ cups water

Preheat oven to 450 degrees. Trim any excess fat from meat. Make a lengthwise cut along the center of the tenderloin, but not all the way through (about ⅓ way down), set aside. In a skillet coated with nonstick cooking spray, sauté the onion and garlic until tender, about 5 minutes. Add the spinach and cook just until the spinach is wilted, stirring constantly, about 1 minute. Remove from the heat and stir in the bread crumbs and cheese. Season to taste. Spread the spinach mixture in the slit of the meat. Squeeze loosely together. Cover the top of the stuffing on the tenderloin loosely with foil. Place cut side up in a roasting pan. Season the meat with salt, pepper and garlic powder. Pour the Worcestershire sauce over. Cook for 40 to 45 minutes for medium rare or to desired doneness. In a microwave dish heat together the bouillon cube, water, and any drippings from the meat for 2 minutes. Slice the tenderloin and pour the sauce over.

Makes 18 to 20 servings

Healthier Approach:
Limit cooked serving size to 3 ounces (size of a deck of cards). Enjoy larger servings of a variety of fresh vegetables and grains.

NUTRITIONAL INFORMATION PER SERVING

Calories	250	Saturated Fat (g)	4
Protein (g)	33	Dietary Fiber (g)	0
Carbohydrate (g)	3	Sodium (mg)	250
Fat (g)	11	Cholesterol (mg)	97
Cal. from Fat (%)	39		

Easy Pot Roast

Throw the roast in the oven, forget about it and cook on a low temperature all day. You can reduce temperature to 250° and leave in oven longer. Wait until you taste the wonderful gravy - be sure to have rice. The perfect recipe for the busy person.

1   (4-pound) beef sirloin tip roast
6   cloves garlic, sliced or garlic
     powder
Salt and pepper to taste
1   large onion, sliced

1   (14-ounce) can low-fat cream
     of mushroom soup
1   (16-ounce) package baby
     carrots

Preheat oven to 300 degrees. Trim any excess fat from meat. Stuff pieces of garlic throughout the meat. Season the meat very well with salt and pepper. Spread the sliced onion over the roast and pour soup over onions. Cover and place in oven for 5 to 6 hours depending on the size of the roast. After 4 hours, add carrots and continue cooking until meat is tender or you're ready for the roast.

Makes 12 to 14 servings

Healthier Approach:

Pour gravy into a "gravy separator," a pitcher-type cup that allows fat to separate from gravy and to be poured off. Sirloin is a lean cut of beef.

NUTRITIONAL INFORMATION PER SERVING

Calories	256	Saturated Fat (g)	3
Protein (g)	38	Dietary Fiber (g)	1
Carbohydrate (g)	6	Sodium (mg)	286
Fat (g)	8	Cholesterol (mg)	106
Cal. from Fat (%)	28		

Tasty Beef Strips

*My daughter brought friends to spend the night and said
"we want something good to eat." I threw together this kid-pleaser
dish and my son used bread to get all of the wonderful sauce.*

2 pounds sirloin strips
(1x1x½-inch pieces)
Garlic powder to taste
Salt and pepper to taste
1 red bell pepper, seeded and
cut into strips

1 (10-ounce) can diced
tomatoes and green chiles
1 cup beef broth
1 (15¼-ounce) can corn, drained
1 (16-ounce) package rotini pasta
Grated Parmesan cheese, optional

Trim any excess fat from the meat. Season heavily with the garlic powder, salt, and pepper. In a large skillet coated with nonstick cooking spray over a medium-high heat, cook the meat and red pepper for about 5 minutes or until the meat is brown. Add the tomatoes, beef broth, and corn. Bring to a boil, reduce the heat and continue cooking for 5 to 7 minutes. Meanwhile, prepare the pasta according to the package directions omitting any oil or salt. Drain and serve meat and sauce over pasta. Sprinkle with Parmesan cheese, if desired.

Makes 8 servings

Healthier Approach:
Serve over a whole grain, such as brown rice, bulgur, or quinoa.

NUTRITIONAL INFORMATION PER SERVING

Calories	456	Saturated Fat (g)	2
Protein (g)	42	Dietary Fiber (g)	3
Carbohydrate (g)	55	Sodium (mg)	465
Fat (g)	7	Cholesterol (mg)	92
Cal. from Fat (%)	15		

Eggplant Bake with Beef

Lots of eggplant, a little beef. With the
marinara and cheese, you have a winner.

6	cups chopped peeled eggplant	½	teaspoon dried basil
1	onion, chopped		Salt and pepper to taste
1	teaspoon minced garlic	3	cups cooked rice
½	pound ground sirloin	2	cups marinara sauce
1	teaspoon dried oregano	1	cup shredded part-skim mozzarella cheese

Preheat oven to 350 degrees. In a large skillet coated with nonstick cooking spray, sauté the eggplant, onion, garlic and ground meat until meat is done and eggplant tender, about 20 minutes. Add the oregano, basil, salt, pepper, and rice, mixing well. Transfer to a 2-quart casserole dish. Cover with marinara sauce and sprinkle with cheese. Bake for 20 to 30 minutes or until thoroughly heated.

Makes 8 servings

Healthier Approach:
Add less ground meat and more veggies, such as diced green/red pepper and zucchini, if desired.

NUTRITIONAL INFORMATION PER SERVING

Calories	243	Saturated Fat (g)	3
Protein (g)	16	Dietary Fiber (g)	3
Carbohydrate (g)	29	Sodium (mg)	425
Fat (g)	7	Cholesterol (mg)	33
Cal. from Fat (%)	27		

Barbecued Brisket

*Here's an easy way to enjoy barbecue. Place in the
oven and later that day, you have sensational barbecue.
This recipe works great in a slow cooker, also.*

1	(5-pound) beef brisket	½ cup vinegar
Salt and lots of pepper to taste		½ cup light brown sugar
1	teaspoon garlic powder	½ cup ketchup
½	cup liquid smoke	½ cup Worcestershire sauce

Trim excess fat from brisket. Season brisket with salt, pepper, and garlic
powder. Mix liquid smoke, vinegar, sugar, ketchup, and Worcestershire sauce
together and spread over brisket. Cover and refrigerate overnight. Preheat
oven to 300 degrees. Place brisket and marinade in oven. Bake, covered, for
4 to 5 hours or until brisket is tender.

Makes 14 to 16 servings

Healthier Approach:
*Prepare day before serving and refrigerate. Remove top layer of hardened
fat before slicing. Rewarm and serve.*

NUTRITIONAL INFORMATION PER SERVING

Calories	256	Saturated Fat (g)	2
Protein (g)	36	Dietary Fiber (g)	0
Carbohydrate (g)	10	Sodium (mg)	248
Fat (g)	7	Cholesterol (mg)	108
Cal. from Fat (%)	26		

Italian Pork Chops

These well-seasoned pork chops produce a delicious gravy, which was super served over rice. This is a great dish because you throw all the ingredients in a pan and place in the oven.

4	pounds center cut pork chops (about 8)	1	large green bell pepper, seeded and sliced into rings
2	tablespoons garlic powder	1	onion, sliced into rings and separated
½	teaspoon pepper		
1	tablespoon dried oregano	4	Roma tomatoes, sliced
1	tablespoon dried basil	1	cup shredded part-skim mozzarella cheese
¼	cup lemon juice		
¼	cup Worcestershire sauce		

Preheat oven to 350 degrees. Trim any fat around the pork chops. Combine together the garlic powder, pepper, oregano, and basil and sprinkle on both sides of the pork chops. Place in an oblong 3-quart baking dish coated with nonstick cooking spray. Combine the lemon juice and Worcestershire sauce and pour over the seasoned pork chops. Lay the green pepper and onion rings on top. Cover and bake for 1 hour to 1 hour, 15 minutes or until the meat is tender. Remove the cover and top with sliced tomatoes and cheese, continue baking 15 minutes.

Makes 8 servings

NUTRITIONAL INFORMATION PER SERVING

Calories	252	Saturated Fat (g)	4
Protein (g)	33	Dietary Fiber (g)	1
Carbohydrate (g)	6	Sodium (mg)	218
Fat (g)	10	Cholesterol (mg)	85
Cal. from Fat (%)	37		

Pork Stew

The cider gives this stew a great flavor and is super
served over mashed potatoes or Double Mashed Potatoes.

3   pounds pork tenderloin, cut
    into 1-inch cubes
Salt and pepper to taste
⅓   cup all-purpose flour
2   large onions, halved and
    thinly sliced

3   cups apple cider
1   (10½-ounce) can beef broth
1   (16-ounce) package baby
    carrots

Heat a large pot coated with nonstick cooking spray over medium-high heat. Add the pork and brown lightly on all sides. Sprinkle the meat with salt and pepper while browning. When all the meat is brown, about 6 minutes, sprinkle with the flour and stir vigorously. Stir in the onions. Cook 3 minutes, stirring constantly. Gradually add the cider and beef broth. Cover and simmer for 1 hour, remove the lid, add carrots, and continue cooking for 20 minutes longer or until the meat is very tender and the carrots are done.

Makes 8 servings

Food Facts:
Pork tenderloin offers a low fat, high protein alternative to other fattier red meat.

NUTRITIONAL INFORMATION PER SERVING

Calories	310	Saturated Fat (g)	2
Protein (g)	38	Dietary Fiber (g)	2
Carbohydrate (g)	24	Sodium (mg)	263
Fat (g)	6	Cholesterol (mg)	111
Cal. from Fat (%)	19		

Glazed Pork Tenderloins

*Here's a quick basic marinade that complements pork.
Keep tenderloins in the freezer and pull out for a
"quickie" dinner. Grill or cook in the oven.*

2 (1-pound) pork tenderloins	2 tablespoons honey
⅓ cup molasses	2 tablespoons Worcestershire
⅓ cup reduced-sodium soy sauce	sauce

Trim tenderloins of excess fat. Combine the molasses, soy sauce, honey, and Worcestershire sauce in a shallow dish with the tenderloins. Cover and refrigerate several hours or overnight, turning several times. Grill pork over medium hot grill for about 20 minutes or until internal temperature is 160 degrees. To prepare in oven, bake at 350 degrees for about 50 minutes.

Makes 8 servings

NUTRITIONAL INFORMATION PER SERVING

Calories	191	Saturated Fat (g)	1
Protein (g)	24	Dietary Fiber (g)	0
Carbohydrate (g)	14	Sodium (mg)	698
Fat (g)	4	Cholesterol (mg)	74
Cal. from Fat (%)	19		

Veal Scaloppine

With this rich flavored sauce, you'll think you're dining in a fine restaurant. You are removing ingredients from the pan, but remember, it's still the same pan. Great with pasta.

1½ pounds thinly sliced veal
(scaloppine)
⅓ cup all-purpose flour
Salt and pepper to taste
½ pound mushrooms, thinly
sliced
1½ tablespoons olive oil

1 onion, chopped
1 tablespoon chopped parsley
½ teaspoon minced garlic
1 teaspoon dried tarragon
1 (10½-ounce) can beef broth
plus ½ cup beef broth
3 tablespoons tomato paste

Cut the veal into serving pieces. Combine the flour, salt, and pepper. Dredge the veal in the flour and set aside. In a large skillet coated with nonstick cooking spray, sauté the mushrooms until tender, about 5 minutes. Remove the mushrooms to a platter. In the same skillet, heat the olive oil. Add the veal pieces and brown on both sides, about 6 minutes. Remove the veal to a plate and set aside. In the same skillet, again coated with nonstick cooking spray, sauté the onion, parsley, and garlic until tender, about 5 minutes. Add the tarragon, beef broth, and tomato paste. Cook over low heat for 10 minutes, scraping pan. Return the mushrooms and veal to the pan and heat thoroughly.

Makes 6 servings

NUTRITIONAL INFORMATION PER SERVING

Calories	237	Saturated Fat (g)	3
Protein (g)	27	Dietary Fiber (g)	1
Carbohydrate (g)	10	Sodium (mg)	387
Fat (g)	9	Cholesterol (mg)	103
Cal. from Fat (%)	36		

Veal Roll-Ups

A pleasing presentation with a
wonderful sauce to please your palate.

2   pounds thinly sliced veal
    (scaloppine)
Salt and pepper to taste
8   slices reduced-fat Swiss
    cheese
1   (10-ounce) package frozen
    chopped spinach, thawed,
    and drained well

2   large egg whites
2   tablespoons skim milk
1   cup seasoned bread crumbs
1   cup beef broth
1   tablespoon lemon juice
1   teaspoon minced garlic

Preheat oven to 350 degrees. Cut veal into eight servings and salt and pepper. On each slice of veal place a cheese slice and evenly spread spinach. Roll each jelly roll fashion and secure with a toothpick. In a small bowl, mix together the egg whites and milk. Dip each roll in milk mixture and then coat with bread crumbs. Place seam side down in an oblong baking dish. Mix together in a bowl the beef broth, lemon juice, and minced garlic. Pour into dish with veal. Cover with foil and bake one hour. Uncover and continue baking for 20 minutes or until veal is tender.

Makes 8 servings

Healthier Approach:
To cut sodium, use lower salt broth and plain bread crumbs.

NUTRITIONAL INFORMATION PER SERVING

Calories	304	Saturated Fat (g)	4
Protein (g)	41	Dietary Fiber (g)	2
Carbohydrate (g)	14	Sodium (mg)	700
Fat (g)	8	Cholesterol (mg)	133
Cal. from Fat (%)	26		

Veal, Mushroom, and Broccoli with Tomato Vinaigrette

A divine one dish meal that is hearty enough to satisfy the men yet light enough to be entertaining. I included pasta but wild rice would be great too.

2   cups broccoli florets
1½ pounds thinly sliced veal
     (scaloppine)
1   tablespoon dried rosemary
Salt and pepper to taste
¼   cup all-purpose flour
2   tablespoons olive oil
½   pound mushrooms, sliced
½   cup sliced green onions
     (scallions)

1½ cups canned fat-free chicken
     broth
2   teaspoons cornstarch
1   tablespoon water
1   tablespoon balsamic vinegar
1   teaspoon Dijon mustard
2   cups chopped Roma (plum)
     tomatoes
1   (12-ounce) package angel hair
     pasta
2   tablespoons chopped parsley

In a microwaveproof dish, cook the broccoli in ½ cup water until crisp-tender, about 5 to 7 minutes. Drain water; set aside. Sprinkle the veal with rosemary, salt and pepper, and then dust with flour. In a large skillet coated with nonstick cooking spray, heat the olive oil over a medium-high heat, add the veal and sauté for about 1 minute per side. Add the mushrooms and cook for 3 to 5 minutes or until the mushrooms are tender. Add the green onions and chicken broth. In a small cup, blend together the cornstarch and water and add to the pan, cooking and stirring until the sauce is thickened. Stir in the vinegar and mustard and cook for 30 seconds. Add the tomatoes and broccoli, cooking until heated through. Meanwhile, prepare the pasta according to the package directions omitting salt and oil. Drain and toss with the parsley. Serve the veal and sauce over the angel hair.

Makes 6 servings

NUTRITIONAL INFORMATION PER SERVING

Calories	450	Saturated Fat (g)	3
Protein (g)	41	Dietary Fiber (g)	3
Carbohydrate (g)	43	Sodium (mg)	375
Fat (g)	13	Cholesterol (mg)	124
Cal. from Fat (%)	25		

Lamb Stew

*Lamb, combined with the squash and mushrooms,
is a great alternative to the traditional stew. The rosemary
adds that finishing touch. Serve over rice.*

1½ pounds lean boneless lamb,
cut into ½-inch pieces
1 large onion, sliced
1 teaspoon minced garlic
1 (14½-ounce) can diced
tomatoes, with their own
juice
1 cup thinly sliced carrot

⅓ cup white wine or chicken
broth
1 tablespoon dried rosemary
1 bay leaf
2 cups cubed yellow squash
(about 2 medium)
½ pound mushrooms, sliced

In a large pot coated with nonstick cooking spray, over a medium-high heat, add the lamb, onion, and garlic, cooking 5 minutes or until the lamb is lightly browned on all sides. Drain any excess grease. Add the tomatoes, carrot, white wine, rosemary, and bay leaf. Bring the mixture to a boil over a medium heat; cover, reduce the heat and simmer for 20 minutes or until the lamb is tender. Stir in the yellow squash and sliced mushrooms, cooking for 15 minutes or until the vegetables are tender. Remove and discard the bay leaf.

Makes 6 servings

Healthier Approach:
Decrease lamb to 1 pound, increase vegetables accordingly.

NUTRITIONAL INFORMATION PER SERVING

Calories	245	Saturated Fat (g)	4
Protein (g)	26	Dietary Fiber (g)	3
Carbohydrate (g)	11	Sodium (mg)	253
Fat (g)	11	Cholesterol (mg)	82
Cal. from Fat (%)	39		

Black Bean and Caramelized Onion Burritos

The flavor of the caramelized onion
is superb combined with the black beans.

3 cups thinly sliced red onion
2 teaspoons sugar
¼ teaspoon dried thyme
1 (15-ounce) can black beans,
  rinsed and drained
½ teaspoon ground cumin

1 cup shredded reduced-fat
  Cheddar cheese
¼ cup minced fresh cilantro,
  optional
8 (6-inch) flour tortillas
Salsa

Preheat oven to 350 degrees. Coat a large skillet with nonstick cooking spray and heat over medium high heat. Add the onion and sugar; sauté 5 minutes or until tender. Reduce heat to medium; continue cooking for 10 to 15 minutes or until the onion is caramelized or deep gold brown. Remove from heat and stir in the thyme. In a mixing bowl, combine the beans, cumin, cheese, and cilantro; stir well. Spoon the bean mixture evenly down the center of each tortilla. Top evenly with the onion mixture. Roll up the tortillas jelly roll style and place the rolls, seam side down, on a baking sheet coated with nonstick cooking spray. Cover and bake for 12 to 15 minutes or until the cheese melts. Serve with salsa.

Makes 8 tortillas

Healthier Approach:
Try whole wheat flour tortillas. Rinse beans before adding to mixing bowl to lower sodium. Add leftover baked sweet potatoes for added nutrition.

NUTRITIONAL INFORMATION PER SERVING

Calories	236	Saturated Fat (g)	1
Protein (g)	11	Dietary Fiber (g)	4
Carbohydrate (g)	39	Sodium (mg)	592
Fat (g)	4	Cholesterol (mg)	3
Cal. from Fat (%)	17		

Pasta with Black Beans

*Vegetarian lovers as well as pasta lovers will put this one
high on their list. I couldn't quit eating it - oh well, it was light!*

1 (8-ounce) package shell-type pasta	1 (15-ounce) can black beans, drained and rinsed
1 tablespoon olive oil	Salt and pepper to taste
1½ teaspoons minced garlic	1 cup chopped Roma (plum) tomatoes
1 bunch green onions (scallions), thinly sliced	
1 teaspoon ground cumin	2 tablespoons chopped fresh cilantro
2 tablespoons lime juice	

Prepare the pasta according to the package directions, omitting oil and salt. Drain; set aside. Meanwhile, heat the olive oil in a medium saucepan over medium heat. Add the garlic, green onions, and cumin and sauté for 2 minutes. Add the lime juice, black beans, salt, pepper, tomatoes, and cilantro, stirring until just heated. Remove from heat, toss with the pasta, and serve.

Makes 4 servings

Food Facts:

This can be served over brown rice or couscous instead of pasta.

NUTRITIONAL INFORMATION PER SERVING

Calories	345	Saturated Fat (g)	1
Protein (g)	14	Dietary Fiber (g)	8
Carbohydrate (g)	62	Sodium (mg)	340
Fat (g)	5	Cholesterol (mg)	0
Cal. from Fat (%)	14		

Southwestern Pasta

Cilantro gives this sensational Southwestern dish a distinct flavor; however, it can be left out if you're not fond of cilantro. If finding the colored bell peppers troubles you, use what is available; just make the dish. Serve with reduced-fat Monterey Jack cheese, if desired.

¼ cup olive oil
1 tablespoon minced garlic
1 red bell pepper, seeded and chopped
1 yellow bell pepper, seeded and chopped
4 Roma (plum) tomatoes, chopped
1 (16-ounce) bag frozen corn

1 tablespoon finely chopped jalapeño pepper
¼ cup chopped fresh cilantro
1 bunch green onions (scallions), chopped
¼ cup lime juice
Salt and pepper to taste
¼ teaspoon ground cumin
1 teaspoon dried oregano
1 (16-ounce) package linguine

In a large skillet, heat the olive oil over a medium heat. Add the garlic and red and yellow peppers and sauté until tender, about 5 minutes. Add the tomatoes, corn, jalapeño pepper, cilantro, green onions, lime juice, salt, pepper, cumin, and oregano, stirring until well heated. Meanwhile, cook the pasta according to the package directions, omitting oil and salt. Drain and add to the skillet, tossing to mix well.

Makes 6 to 8 servings

NUTRITIONAL INFORMATION PER SERVING

Calories	295	Saturated Fat (g)	1
Protein (g)	9	Dietary Fiber (g)	4
Carbohydrate (g)	51	Sodium (mg)	111
Fat (g)	9	Cholesterol (mg)	0
Cal. from Fat (%)	25		

Tortellini Primavera

*Tortellini combined with the veggies gives this
Primavera a new dimension. Top it off with the white
sauce and your dish is a creamy winner.*

2 (6-ounce) packages cheese
  filled tortellini
3 cups carrot strips
  (3 inches long)
1 tablespoon minced garlic
3 cups zucchini strips
  (3 inches long)
1 red bell pepper, seeded and
  cut into 3-inch strips
1 (6-ounce) package frozen
  snow peas

1 bunch green onions
  (scallions) sliced
2 cups chopped Roma (plum)
  tomatoes
½ teaspoon crushed red pepper
  flakes
⅓ cup grated Parmesan cheese
¼ cup all-purpose flour
2½ cups skim milk
Salt and pepper to taste

Prepare the tortellini according to the package directions, omitting oil and salt. Drain; set aside. In a large skillet coated with nonstick cooking spray, sauté the carrots, garlic, zucchini, and bell pepper until tender, about 8 minutes. Add the snow peas, green onions, tomatoes, and crushed red pepper, cooking until crisp-tender, about 5 minutes. Stir in the cooked tortellini and Parmesan cheese. Meanwhile, combine the flour and milk together in a saucepan. Cook over medium heat until thickened; salt and pepper to taste. Pour over the tortellini vegetable mixture, toss gently, and serve.

Makes 6 servings

Food Facts:

A variety of colors in your vegetable choices, as in this recipe, usually means a large variety of protective nutrients and phytochemicals.

NUTRITIONAL INFORMATION PER SERVING

Calories	350	Saturated Fat (g)	4
Protein (g)	18	Dietary Fiber (g)	7
Carbohydrate (g)	55	Sodium (mg)	379
Fat (g)	7	Cholesterol (mg)	27
Cal. from Fat (%)	17		

Roasted Pepper and Spinach Penne

The combination of these ingredients makes a palate-pleasing pasta dish. I know some of these ingredients might not be in your pantry but it's worth the purchase for the dish. Seafood or chicken can be added, but it's hard to beat like this.

1 (16-ounce) package penne (tubular) pasta	1 (7-ounce) jar roasted red pepper, packed in water, drained and sliced
1 (10-ounce) package frozen leaf spinach, thawed and drained	1 teaspoon dried basil
¼ cup olive oil	1 teaspoon dried oregano
1½ cups chopped red onion	Salt and pepper to taste
1 tablespoon minced garlic	2 tablespoons capers, drained
	2 tablespoons pine nuts

Prepare pasta according to directions; drain. Cook the spinach according to package directions. In a large skillet, heat the olive oil and sauté the onion and garlic until tender, 5 minutes. Add the roasted pepper, spinach, basil, and oregano. Add the pasta, season with salt and pepper, and toss with the capers and pine nuts.

Makes 8 to 10 side dish servings

Makes 4 to 6 main dish servings

Food Facts:

Red peppers are a good source of carotenoids and flavonoids, so they can play a role in fighting off cancer, heart disease, and stroke.

NUTRITIONAL INFORMATION PER MAIN DISH SERVING

Calories	420	Saturated Fat (g)	2
Protein (g)	13	Dietary Fiber (g)	4
Carbohydrate (g)	65	Sodium (mg)	198
Fat (g)	12	Cholesterol (mg)	0
Cal. from Fat (%)	26		

Pasta with Broccoli and Beans

Here's a super meatless entrée that has lots of character.

1	(16-ounce) package penne pasta	3	tablespoons olive oil
8	cups broccoli florets	1	(16-ounce) can cannellini beans, undrained
1	red bell pepper, seeded and cut into strips		Salt and pepper to taste
1	tablespoon minced garlic	⅓	cup grated Parmesan cheese

Cook pasta according package directions omitting any oil and salt; drain. In a large skillet, stir-fry broccoli, red pepper strips, and garlic in oil until veggies are crisp and tender, about 8 minutes. Add beans with their liquid, salt, pepper, and pasta to broccoli; heat through. Toss with cheese and serve.

Makes 6 servings

Food Facts:

Beans of all kinds offer a hefty dose of dietary fiber. In fact, one (½-cup) serving can provide one-third of the daily recommendation of 20 to 35 grams. Broccoli includes phytochemicals (sulforaphane, indoles, and isothiocyanates) that studies say can protect against cancer.

NUTRITIONAL INFORMATION PER SERVING

Calories	418	Saturated Fat (g)	2
Protein (g)	18	Dietary Fiber (g)	8
Carbohydrate (g)	74	Sodium (mg)	291
Fat (g)	6	Cholesterol (mg)	4
Cal. from Fat (%)	12		

Pesto Pasta

Use fresh basil to properly enjoy this dish.
The leftovers served cold made a great salad the next day.

¼ cup chopped fresh basil
1 teaspoon minced garlic
3 tablespoons balsamic vinegar
2 tablespoons chopped flat-leaf parsley
2 tablespoons lemon juice
3 tablespoons olive oil

4 cups coarsely chopped tomatoes
1 (16-ounce) package fettuccine
3 tablespoons grated Romano cheese
3 tablespoons pine nuts, toasted

In a food processor, process basil, garlic, vinegar, parsley, and lemon juice. With machine running, slowly add olive oil in a steady stream until thickened. Add tomatoes; process 5 seconds. Place sauce in a large bowl. Cook pasta according to package directions, omitting oil and salt. Drain and add to sauce. Add cheese and pine nuts and toss well.

Makes 6 servings

Food Facts:
Pesto can also be made with a combination of olive oil, basil, Romano cheese, and spinach. A nice (and healthful) change.

NUTRITIONAL INFORMATION PER SERVING

Calories	335	Saturated Fat (g)	2
Protein (g)	11	Dietary Fiber (g)	4
Carbohydrate (g)	51	Sodium (mg)	186
Fat (g)	12	Cholesterol (mg)	3
Cal. from Fat (%)	30		

Summer Veggie Pasta

If you have a garden, this recipe is like a gift at the end of the summer. Unfortunately, I don't, so I stick to the grocery stores or my nice friends bring me veggies from their gardens. Throw in your favorite veggies.

3	tablespoons olive oil	1	zucchini or yellow squash, thinly sliced
1	teaspoon minced garlic	1	bunch green onions (scallions), chopped
1	tomato, chopped	1	teaspoon dried basil
1	red bell pepper, seeded and chopped	1	teaspoon dried oregano
1	green bell pepper, seeded and chopped	1	(16-ounce) package ziti pasta
1	eggplant, peeled and chopped		Salt and pepper to taste

In a large pan coated with nonstick cooking spray, heat the olive oil and sauté the garlic, tomato, bell peppers, eggplant, squash, green onions, basil, and oregano until tender. Meanwhile cook the ziti according to package directions, omitting any oil and salt. Drain and toss with the sautéed vegetables. Season to taste with salt and pepper.

Makes 8 servings.

Food Facts:
Enjoy the late summer harvest by frequenting your local farmers' market. And be creative…the vegetables here are only suggestions. Use whatever is on sale or looks especially fresh this week!

NUTRITIONAL INFORMATION PER SERVING

Calories	290	Saturated Fat (g)	1
Protein (g)	9	Dietary Fiber (g)	4
Carbohydrate (g)	50	Sodium (mg)	10
Fat (g)	6	Cholesterol (mg)	0
Cal. from Fat (%)	19		

Southwestern Spinach Lasagne

This easily layered dish is a
nice alternative to traditional lasagne.

1 tablespoon margarine	1 (10-ounce) can tomato and
1 onion, chopped	green chiles, drained
1 cup skim milk	Salt and pepper to taste
2 tablespoons all-purpose flour	10 tortillas
1 (10-ounce) package frozen	2 cups shredded reduced-fat
chopped spinach, thawed	Monterey Jack cheese
	1 cup fat-free sour cream

Preheat oven to 350 degrees. In a nonstick skillet coated with nonstick cooking spray, melt margarine and sauté onion until tender. In a small bowl, mix together the milk and flour and add to sautéed onion. Cook over medium heat until thickened. Meanwhile, cook spinach according to package directions, drain well. Add spinach and tomatoes and continue heating until thick. Season with salt and pepper to taste. In a 2-quart baking dish, layer tortillas, spinach layer, cheese, and sour cream; repeating layers. Bake 30 minutes or until cheese melts.

Makes 8 servings

Food Facts:
Spinach is a good source of beta carotene and Vitamin C.

Healthier Approach:
Throw in some other veggies that complement spinach such as mushrooms or white beans.

NUTRITIONAL INFORMATION PER SERVING

Calories	338		
Protein (g)	17	Dietary Fiber (g)	2
Carbohydrate (g)	44	Sodium (mg)	846
Fat (g)	10	Cholesterol (mg)	16
Cal. from Fat (%)	28		
Saturated Fat (g)	4		

Veggie Paella

This deceptively easy recipe boasts lots of flavor and color.

2 tablespoons olive oil
1 cup chopped onion
1 red bell pepper, seeded and chopped
1 cup sliced mushrooms
1 teaspoon minced garlic
1 (16-ounce) package yellow rice

4 cups water
1 cup chopped tomatoes
1 (15-ounce) can black beans, drained and rinsed
1 (10-ounce) package frozen peas, thawed
½ teaspoon paprika
1 teaspoon dried basil

In a large pot, heat oil and sauté onion, red pepper, mushrooms, and garlic about 5 to 7 minutes. Add rice and water and bring to a boil. Reduce heat, cover, and cook for 20 to 25 minutes or until rice is done. Stir in tomato, black beans, peas, paprika, and basil until well heated.

Makes 8 servings

Healthier Approach:
This dish can accommodate a variety of vegetables, as well as a potpourri of beans, corn, and chopped fresh herbs. Rinse beans to lower sodium.

NUTRITIONAL INFORMATION PER SERVING

Calories	303	Saturated Fat (g)	1
Protein (g)	9	Dietary Fiber (g)	6
Carbohydrate (g)	59	Sodium (mg)	1106
Fat (g)	4	Cholesterol (mg)	0
Cal. from Fat (%)	12		

Veggie Au Gratin

Veggies, white sauce, and cheese make this a vegetarian favorite meal or it makes a great side.

4   large red potatoes, sliced (about 1½ pounds)
¾   pound green beans, ends snapped
1   pound yellow squash, sliced
Salt and pepper to taste

1½ cups shredded reduced-fat Cheddar cheese, divided
1   cup frozen green peas, thawed
2   cups skim milk
⅓   cup all-purpose flour

Preheat oven to 350 degrees. Cook potatoes, green beans, and squash in a little water in microwave or on stove until crisp-tender. Spread potatoes in bottom of a 2-quart casserole coated with nonstick cooking spray and sprinkle with salt and pepper and ¾ cup cheese. Top with green beans. Layer squash and peas on top. In a small pan combine milk and flour and heat until thickened. Pour over the top of layered veggies. Top with remaining ¾ cup cheese. Bake for 20 minutes or until heated through.

Makes 4 to 6 servings

Food Facts:
Green beans are a good source of quercetin, a flavonoid that may help fight cancer, heart disease, and stroke.

NUTRITIONAL INFORMATION PER SERVING

Calories	290	Saturated Fat (g)	1
Protein (g)	17	Dietary Fiber (g)	8
Carbohydrate (g)	52	Sodium (mg)	253
Fat (g)	3	Cholesterol (mg)	7
Cal. from Fat (%)	8		

Cheesy Eggplant Casserole

*Eggplant lovers will really enjoy this quick
version of an eggplant Parmesan in casserole form.
You can use mozzarella cheese, if desired.*

1 (1-pound) eggplant, peeled and cut into ½-inch cubes	3 slices reduced-fat American cheese, cut into strips
1½ cups chopped onion	1 (8-ounce) can tomato sauce
1 cup chopped green bell pepper	1 cup soft bread crumbs

Preheat the oven to 375 degrees. In a pot coated with nonstick cooking spray, sauté the eggplant, onion, and green pepper, covered, stirring often, until tender, about 15 minutes. Place the eggplant mixture in the bottom of a 1½-quart casserole. Place cheese strips on top of the eggplant. Pour the tomato sauce on top and sprinkle with bread crumbs. Bake for 30 minutes or until the casserole is bubbly.

Makes 4 servings

Food Facts:

Eggplant is a very low calorie vegetable that is high in anthycyanosides, antioxidants that help fight cancer and heart disease.

Healthier Approach:

Use "no salt added" tomato sauce, if desired.

NUTRITIONAL INFORMATION PER SERVING

Calories	224	Saturated Fat (g)	1
Protein (g)	12	Dietary Fiber (g)	6
Carbohydrate (g)	39	Sodium (mg)	886
Fat (g)	3	Cholesterol (mg)	7
Cal. from Fat (%)	13		

Stuffed Potatoes Primavera

These colorful tasty potatoes also make a great side:
cut potato in half and fill. Freezes well.

6 medium baking potatoes	2 cups small broccoli florets
½ cup skim milk	2 cups coarsely chopped yellow
2 tablespoons margarine or	squash
butter	1 cup coarsely chopped green
Salt and pepper to taste	bell pepper
½ cup chopped green onions	1 cup coarsely chopped onions
(scallions)	1 cup chopped tomatoes
1½ cups shredded part-skim	¼ cup balsamic vinegar
mozzarella cheese	1 teaspoon dried basil

Preheat oven to 400 degrees. Wash and scrub potatoes. Bake for 1 hour or until soft when squeezed. When done, cut thin slice off top of potato lengthwise. Scoop out the potato pulp leaving the shell. In a mixing bowl, blend together the potato pulp, milk, and margarine until creamy. Season with salt and pepper to taste. Stir in the green onions and mozzarella cheese. Reduce oven to 350 degrees. Meanwhile, in a large pan coated with nonstick cooking spray, sauté the broccoli, squash, green pepper, onions, tomatoes, vinegar, and basil over medium heat for 7 to 10 minutes or until the vegetables are tender. Carefully fold the vegetables into the potato mixture. Stuff the potato shells with the mixture. Place on a baking sheet and bake for 15 to 20 minutes or until well heated and the cheese is melted.

Makes 6 main dish servings

Healthier Approach:
Add any vegetables available - often, the more colorful the array of veggies, the more healthful.

NUTRITIONAL INFORMATION PER SERVING

Calories	304	Saturated Fat (g)	4
Protein (g)	15	Dietary Fiber (g)	6
Carbohydrate (g)	43	Sodium (mg)	305
Fat (g)	10	Cholesterol (mg)	16
Cal. from Fat (%)	27		

Corny Rice

The hint of cumin in this colorful dish gives it a Southwestern touch.
Corn and rice are two popular sides so together you have a hit!

1   cup green onions (scallions),   Salt and pepper to taste
    thinly sliced   ½   cup canned fat-free chicken
1   (16-ounce) package frozen   broth
    corn, thawed   3   cups cooked brown rice
½   teaspoon ground cumin   ¼   cup chopped parsley

In a large pan coated with nonstick cooking spray, sauté the green onions for
several minutes. Add corn, cumin, salt, pepper, and chicken broth. Continue
cooking until the corn is done, about 2 minutes. Stir in the rice and parsley and
continue cooking until heated through, about 3 minutes.

Makes 6 servings

Food Facts:
Brown rice offers extra fiber and lots of B vitamins. Filling, too!

NUTRITIONAL INFORMATION PER SERVING

Calories	177	Saturated Fat (g)	0
Protein (g)	5	Dietary Fiber (g)	4
Carbohydrate (g)	39	Sodium (mg)	27
Fat (g)	1	Cholesterol (mg)	0
Cal. from Fat (%)	6		

Holiday Rice Pilaf

When you are out of oven space, here is the perfect holiday side dish.
The red and green color with the toasted pecan nutty flavor makes
this a special dish; don't save it only for the holidays.

2	(16-ounce) cans fat-free chicken broth (4 cups)	½	cup sliced green onions (scallions)
2	cups rice	1	teaspoon minced garlic
1	tablespoon margarine	½	pound mushrooms, sliced
⅓	cup chopped pecans	1	cup chopped red bell pepper
		1	cup frozen green peas, thawed

In a large saucepan, bring the chicken broth to a boil; stir in the rice. Return to a boil. Reduce heat, cover, and cook for about 20 minutes or until the rice is done. Meanwhile, in a large skillet, melt the margarine and add the pecans. Cook the pecans for 2 to 3 minutes, stirring constantly. Add the green onions, garlic, mushrooms, and red pepper sautéing for 5 minutes or until the vegetables are tender. Add the peas to the mixture, stirring until heated through. Add the cooked rice to the pecan mixture tossing until well combined.

Makes 8 servings

Healthier Approach:
Substitute quick-cooking brown rice; prepare according to package directions.

NUTRITIONAL INFORMATION PER SERVING

Calories	260	Saturated Fat (g)	1
Protein (g)	9	Dietary Fiber (g)	3
Carbohydrate (g)	44	Sodium (mg)	127
Fat (g)	5	Cholesterol (mg)	0
Cal. from Fat (%)	18		

Rice Primavera

While your rice is cooking, sauté the veggies
and then toss it all together and serve. You can use
whatever type rice you have in the pantry.

2 cups broccoli florets	1 (5-ounce) can evaporated
1 cup sliced mushrooms	skimmed milk
2 cups sliced yellow squash,	4 cups cooked rice
cut in fourths	⅓ cup grated Parmesan cheese
1 cup coarsely chopped onion	Salt and pepper to taste
1 teaspoon minced garlic	¼ teaspoon crushed red pepper
1 cup coarsely chopped	flakes, optional
tomatoes (Roma)	

In a large skillet coated with nonstick cooking spray, stir-fry the broccoli, mushrooms, squash, onion, and garlic for about 7 to 8 minutes or until tender. Add tomatoes and continue cooking for 2 minutes. Stir in evaporated milk and continue cooking until well heated. Add the rice, cheese, salt, pepper, and pepper flakes, cooking and tossing until well mixed and heated.

Makes 6 to 8 servings

Healthier Approach:
Brown rice can be used for additional dietary fiber and trace nutrients.

NUTRITIONAL INFORMATION PER SERVING

Calories	162	Saturated Fat (g)	1
Protein (g)	7	Dietary Fiber (g)	2
Carbohydrate (g)	30	Sodium (mg)	106
Fat (g)	2	Cholesterol (mg)	4
Cal. from Fat (%)	10		

Wild Rice and Pea Casserole

Use a good quality wild rice cooked in chicken broth for an extra touch - a gourmet impression. There are all types of wild rice mixes in the stores.

1 tablespoon olive oil	1 tablespoon Worcestershire
½ pound mushrooms, sliced	sauce
1 onion, chopped	Salt and pepper to taste
4 cups cooked wild rice	¼ cup sliced almonds, toasted,
1 (10-ounce) package frozen	optional
green peas, thawed	

Preheat oven to 325 degrees. In a skillet, heat olive oil and sauté mushrooms and onion until tender, about 5 to 7 minutes. In a 2-quart casserole dish, combine sautéed vegetables, rice, peas, Worcestershire sauce, salt, and pepper. Cover and bake for 20 minutes. Remove from oven and fold in almonds.

Makes 8 to 10 servings

Food Facts:
Green peas are a wonderful addition to both hot and cold rice dishes for color, texture, and nutrition.

NUTRITIONAL INFORMATION PER SERVING

Calories	111	Saturated Fat (g)	0
Protein (g)	5	Dietary Fiber (g)	3
Carbohydrate (g)	20	Sodium (mg)	52
Fat (g)	2	Cholesterol (mg)	0
Cal. from Fat (%)	14		

SIDES

Basic Risotto

Here's a basic recipe for risotto. Add whatever ingredients are hanging around so it will be different each time. I usually clean out my veggies; add cooked veggies toward the end and uncooked earlier. The corn keeps it creamy.

2 teaspoons margarine	4 cups canned fat-free chicken broth
1 teaspoon olive oil	
1 cup chopped onion	1 (15-ounce) can cream style corn
2 cups Arborio rice	
½ cup white wine, optional	¼ cup shredded Romano cheese

In large skillet, heat margarine and oil and sauté onion for 5 minutes or until tender. Add rice and stir for 2 minutes to coat well. Add wine, cooking for 30 seconds. Add broth, ½ cup at a time, stirring constantly until each portion of broth is absorbed before adding next. Add the cream style corn, stirring until mixture is creamy. Add cheese and veggies of your choice, stirring until well heated.

Note: The risotto will cook in about 30 minutes, adding more broth if needed. Risotto is done when rice is tender but firm to bite.

Makes 8 servings

Food Facts:
Arborio rice is a thick, short grain, Italian rice used to prepare risotto.

Healthier Approach:
This basic recipe offers a wonderful opportunity to add a wide variety of chopped vegetables of your choice. Steam vegetables lightly and add when rice is just done.

NUTRITIONAL INFORMATION PER SERVING

Calories	296	Saturated Fat (g)	1
Protein (g)	9	Dietary Fiber (g)	2
Carbohydrate (g)	56	Sodium (mg)	287
Fat (g)	3	Cholesterol (mg)	3
Cal. from Fat (%)	8		

Risotto with Artichokes

*Here's a great recipe to serve with
a beef dish or serve as a meatless entrée.*

½ cup finely chopped onion
1 (14½-ounce) can artichoke
  hearts, drained and sliced
1 tablespoon minced garlic
2 cups Arborio rice

⅓ cup dry white wine or beef
  broth
1 (14½-ounce) can beef broth
Salt and pepper to taste
¼ cup chopped parsley
¼ cup grated Parmesan cheese

In a large skillet coated with nonstick cooking spray, sauté onion several minutes or until it begins to soften. Add artichokes and garlic and continue cooking until onion is tender. Add rice, stir and cook until rice is opaque, 1 to 3 minutes. Add the wine and cook, stirring frequently, until liquid is completely absorbed, about 3 minutes. Heat the beef broth in the microwave until hot. Add ½ cup of the heated broth mixture, stirring frequently, until most of the liquid is absorbed, 3 to 5 minutes. Continue adding remaining broth, ½ cup at a time, letting liquid absorb after each addition, stirring constantly, and cooking until rice is tender and creamy, about 25 minutes. If you need more liquid, use water. When risotto is done, season to taste with salt and pepper. Add parsley and Parmesan cheese. Stir until well blended and serve immediately.

Makes 8 servings

Food Facts:
Artichokes offer a health protective substance called silymarin, which may play a role in cancer prevention.

NUTRITIONAL INFORMATION PER SERVING

Calories	262	Saturated Fat (g)	1
Protein (g)	8	Dietary Fiber (g)	1
Carbohydrate (g)	50	Sodium (mg)	406
Fat (g)	1	Cholesterol (mg)	2
Cal. from Fat (%)	4		

Rice and Pasta Blend

*The golden brown pasta combined with the rice
gives this dish a rich, nutty flavor. If desired, use beef
broth instead of chicken to serve with meat.*

1	tablespoon margarine or butter	2	(14½-ounce) cans fat-free chicken broth
1	tablespoon olive oil	1	cup sliced mushrooms
8	ounces angel hair pasta, broken into small pieces		Salt and pepper to taste
1½	cups rice	2	tablespoons sliced almonds, toasted

In a large saucepan coated with nonstick cooking spray, melt the margarine
and olive oil and sauté the pasta, stirring frequently until golden brown. Add
the rice, broth and mushrooms. Season to taste with salt and pepper. Bring to
a boil, reduce heat and simmer, covered, for 20 minutes or until rice is done.
Transfer to a serving platter and sprinkle with the sliced almonds.

Makes 10 servings

Healthier Approach:
Try brown rice. Sprinkle with chives and/or sliced scallions.

NUTRITIONAL INFORMATION PER SERVING

Calories	207	Saturated Fat (g)	0
Protein (g)	7	Dietary Fiber (g)	1
Carbohydrate (g)	35	Sodium (mg)	152
Fat (g)	4	Cholesterol (mg)	0
Cal. from Fat (%)	16		

Very Good Vermicelli

*When you need a simple pasta side dish with
a little extra pizzazz, try this lightly flavored vermicelli.*

1   (16-ounce) package vermicelli
1½ tablespoons olive oil

½   cup canned fat-free chicken
    broth
1   teaspoon minced garlic

Prepare the pasta according to the package directions. Drain. Toss with the olive oil, chicken broth and garlic, tossing until well mixed and heated through.

Makes 6 to 8 servings

Healthier Approach:
Add frozen peas and chopped red peppers.

NUTRITIONAL INFORMATION PER SERVING

Calories	229	Saturated Fat (g)	1
Protein (g)	8	Dietary Fiber (g)	2
Carbohydrate (g)	42	Sodium (mg)	14
Fat (g)	4	Cholesterol (mg)	0
Cal. from Fat (%)	15		

Poppyseed Pasta

1 tablespoon margarine or butter
1 tablespoon olive oil
2 tablespoons sliced almonds

2 tablespoons poppyseeds
¼ teaspoon salt
1 (16-ounce) package wide noodles

In a saucepan, melt margarine and olive oil and sauté almonds over medium heat, stirring, until golden. Stir in poppyseeds and salt. Meanwhile, cook pasta according to directions on package; drain. Toss pasta with poppyseed mixture, mix lightly.

Makes 8 to 10 servings

Healthier Approach:
Try whole-wheat noodles.

NUTRITIONAL INFORMATION PER SERVING

Calories	212	Saturated Fat (g)	1
Protein (g)	7	Dietary Fiber (g)	1
Carbohydrate (g)	33	Sodium (mg)	25
Fat (g)	6	Cholesterol (mg)	43
Cal. from Fat (%)	25		

Scalloped Potatoes

Here's a way to enjoy an old favorite without guilt.
Sometimes I use Cheddar cheese to top potatoes.

3   pounds red potatoes, peeled
    and sliced into ¼-inch slices
¼   cup all-purpose flour
2   cups skim milk
1   teaspoon minced garlic

Salt and pepper to taste
½   cup reduced-fat shredded
    Swiss cheese
½   cup chopped green onions
    (scallions)

Combine potatoes and enough water to cover in a saucepan; bring to a boil. Cover and cook until tender, about 15 minutes. Do not overcook; drain. In a saucepan, combine the flour, milk, and garlic and cook until thickened, stirring. Season to taste. In an 11x7x2-inch baking pan coated with nonstick cooking spray, place half of the potato slices along the bottom and top with half the milk mixture. Sprinkle each potato layer with salt and pepper. Repeat layers with the potato slices, seasoning, and milk mixture. Bake for 20 minutes. Remove from oven and sprinkle top with Swiss cheese and green onions; continue cooking 5 minutes longer or until cheese is melted.

Makes 8 servings

Healthier Approach:
To add nutrition and color, add green, red, or yellow bell pepper rings.

NUTRITIONAL INFORMATION PER SERVING

Calories	212	Saturated Fat (g)	0
Protein (g)	8	Dietary Fiber (g)	3
Carbohydrate (g)	44	Sodium (mg)	63
Fat (g)	1	Cholesterol (mg)	4
Cal. from Fat (%)	3		

Roasted Potatoes and Onions

This recipe finds its way onto our dinner table often.
I like to use white baking potatoes.

2 pounds baking potatoes (about 3 large), cut into large chunks	1 teaspoon dried oregano
	1 teaspoon dried marjoram
	1 teaspoon minced garlic
2 onions, cut into chunks	Salt and pepper to taste
3 tablespoons olive oil	¼ cup chopped fresh parsley, optional
1 teaspoon dried thyme	

Preheat oven to 450 degrees. Combine the potatoes, onions, olive oil, thyme, oregano, marjoram, and garlic in a large baking pan, tossing well to coat. Bake for 1 hour, stirring every 15 minutes, until the potatoes are crisp and golden brown. Season potatoes with salt and pepper and sprinkle with the parsley.

Makes 6 servings

Food Facts:
Herbs and spices offer important "phytochemicals" or health-protective substances. Enjoy fresh herbs, too, and use a variety for great taste and good health.

Healthier Approach:
Try using half sweet potatoes for a nutritional boost.

NUTRITIONAL INFORMATION PER SERVING

Calories	175	Saturated Fat (g)	1
Protein (g)	4	Dietary Fiber (g)	3
Carbohydrate (g)	31	Sodium (mg)	10
Fat (g)	5	Cholesterol (mg)	0
Cal. from Fat (%)	24		

Smashed Potatoes

*The flavor of the roasted potatoes with garlic
and green onions makes this potato dish hard to beat.*

3	pounds red potatoes, cut in quarters	6	cloves garlic
1	bunch green onions (scallions), cut in thirds	¼	cup margarine or butter
		½	cup fat-free sour cream
			Salt and pepper to taste

Preheat oven to 350 degrees. On a baking sheet coated with nonstick cooking spray, spread the potatoes (peeling on), green onions, and garlic. Coat potatoes with nonstick cooking spray. Bake for 30 minutes, toss the potato mixture and continue baking for 20 minutes or until tender. Transfer all potato mixture to a mixing bowl and mix with margarine and sour cream. Season with salt and pepper.

Makes 8 servings

Healthier Approach:
To cut fat and calories, use a powdered butter substitute (to taste) instead of the margarine or butter.

NUTRITIONAL INFORMATION PER SERVING

Calories	224	Saturated Fat (g)	1
Protein (g)	5	Dietary Fiber (g)	3
Carbohydrate (g)	39	Sodium (mg)	98
Fat (g)	6	Cholesterol (mg)	1
Cal. from Fat (%)	23		

SIDES

Potato Pizza

Instead of mashed or baked potato, try this version.
Adjust the recipe for your family by adding different cheeses or
leaving off the onions...serve with a dollop of fat-free sour cream.

4 baking potatoes, peeled and
   cut into ¼-inch round slices
1 tablespoon minced garlic
2 tablespoons olive oil
Salt and pepper to taste

½ cup chopped green onions
   (scallions)
½ cup shredded reduced-fat
   Cheddar cheese

Preheat oven to 350 degrees. In a large bowl, mix together the potato slices, garlic, olive oil, salt, and pepper. Coat a 12-inch pizza pan with nonstick cooking spray and arrange the potato slices to cover the pizza pan, overlapping the slices. Bake for 35 to 40 minutes or until the potato slices are tender. Remove from the oven and sprinkle with the green onions and cheese. Return to the oven and continue baking for 5 minutes longer or until the cheese is melted.

Makes 6 to 8 servings.

Healthier Approach:
Top with diced fresh tomatoes and green peppers or lightly steamed broccoli florets.

NUTRITIONAL INFORMATION PER SERVING

Calories	120	Saturated Fat (g)	1
Protein (g)	4	Dietary Fiber (g)	1
Carbohydrate (g)	18	Sodium (mg)	48
Fat (g)	4	Cholesterol (mg)	1
Cal. from Fat (%)	29		

Creamed Double Potatoes

A fabulous combo and a way to make our
old time favorite "mashed potatoes" more nutritious.

1¾ pounds sweet potatoes
(yams)
1¾ pounds baking potatoes

2 tablespoons margarine or
butter
⅓ cup skim milk
2 tablespoons honey

In a large pot, cover baking and sweet potatoes with water and bring to a boil for 40 minutes or until tender. Peel the potatoes and place in a mixing bowl with the margarine, blending until smooth. Gradually add the milk and honey, beating until creamy.

Makes 8 to 10 servings

Food Facts:
Yummy way to increase the nutritional value of mashed potatoes. Sweet potatoes are rich in beta carotene, Vitamin C, and Vitamin E.

NUTRITIONAL INFORMATION PER SERVING

Calories	190	Saturated Fat (g)	0
Protein (g)	3	Dietary Fiber (g)	3
Carbohydrate (g)	40	Sodium (mg)	98
Fat (g)	3	Cholesterol (mg)	0
Cal. from Fat (%)	12		

Lemon Sweet Potato Casserole

A quick method to shred sweet potatoes is in the food processor. All the ingredients are combined together, to make this lemon lover's outstanding dish - it's almost like a pudding.

6 cups shredded peeled sweet potatoes (yams), about 3 medium	1 cup skim milk
	2 large eggs
	½ teaspoon ground cinnamon
2 tablespoons margarine or butter, melted	1 (4-serving) box instant lemon pudding and pie filling
⅔ cup sugar	

Preheat oven to 325 degrees. Combine shredded sweet potatoes, margarine, sugar, milk, eggs, cinnamon, and pudding mix in a 2-quart oblong casserole dish. Cover tightly with foil and bake for one hour. Remove foil and continue cooking 20 to 30 minutes longer or until top is golden brown.

Makes 10 to 12 servings

NUTRITIONAL INFORMATION PER SERVING

Calories	288	Saturated Fat (g)	1
Protein (g)	4	Dietary Fiber (g)	3
Carbohydrate (g)	61	Sodium (mg)	194
Fat (g)	3	Cholesterol (mg)	36
Cal. from Fat (%)	10		

Sweet Potato Cranberry Galette

A great opportunity to be the hit of the evening with this outstanding presentation and flavor to match. The dish inverts easily so don't fret about the presentation.

2	tablespoons margarine or butter	¼	cup light brown sugar
1	tablespoon olive oil	1	tablespoon ground ginger
1	cup chopped onion	2-2½	pounds sweet potatoes (yams)
1	cup dried cranberries		

Preheat oven to 400 degrees. In a skillet, heat margarine and olive oil and sauté onions until very tender, about 5 to 7 minutes. Add cranberries, brown sugar, and ginger, stirring until mixed. Line a 9-inch round cake pan with aluminum foil and coat with nonstick cooking spray. Peel potatoes and slice very thin, preferably with a food processor. Spoon one tablespoon of cranberry mixture in center of cake pan. Arrange one-third of the potato slices in concentric circles, overlapping in bottom of pan. Spread half of cranberry mixture over potatoes. Top with another one-third potato slices, arranged in same manner. Top with remaining cranberry mixture and end with potatoes. Coat a sheet of aluminum foil with nonstick cooking spray and cover potatoes tightly. Cook for 40 minutes, uncover and continue baking for an additional 20 minutes or until brown and crisp on top and potatoes are tender. Place serving plate on cake pan and invert.

Makes 8 servings

NUTRITIONAL INFORMATION PER SERVING

Calories	236	Saturated Fat (g)	1
Protein (g)	2	Dietary Fiber (g)	5
Carbohydrate (g)	47	Sodium (mg)	53
Fat (g)	5	Cholesterol (mg)	0
Cal. from Fat (%)	18		

Twice Baked Yams

Yummy, yummy, yummy!
Here's a show piece with the taste to back it up.

3	pounds small, unpeeled sweet potatoes	1	(8-ounce) can crushed pineapple in own juice, drained
½	cup golden raisins	1	teaspoon vanilla extract
1	tablespoon light brown sugar	2	tablespoons chopped pecans
¼	teaspoon ground cinnamon	1	cup miniature marshmallows

Preheat oven to 400 degrees. Place potatoes on a baking sheet. Cook for 1 hour or until tender. Let cool 15 minutes. Cut a thin slice off the top of each potato; carefully scoop pulp into a bowl, leaving shells intact. Mash pulp; stir in raisins, brown sugar, cinnamon, pineapple, and vanilla. Spoon into shells; sprinkle with pecans and marshmallows. Bake at 350 degrees for 15 minutes or until thoroughly heated.

Makes 8 servings

Food Facts:

Sweet potatoes can also be microwaved for a quicker dish. Eat the skin in order to get the most nutrients.

NUTRITIONAL INFORMATION PER SERVING

Calories	189	Saturated Fat (g)	0
Protein (g)	3	Dietary Fiber (g)	4
Carbohydrate (g)	43	Sodium (mg)	15
Fat (g)	1	Cholesterol (mg)	0
Cal. from Fat (%)	7		

Spinach and Corn Casserole

IDES

*This combination makes an extremely tasty as well as
colorful dish. You might want to double this recipe
because people will ask for seconds.*

1 (10-ounce) package frozen chopped spinach	¼ cup bread crumbs
½ cup chopped onion	1 tablespoon grated Parmesan cheese
1 (15-ounce) can cream style corn	1 tablespoon margarine or butter, melted, or olive oil

Preheat oven to 400 degrees. Cook the spinach according to package directions; drain very well. In a small skillet, coated with nonstick cooking spray, sauté the onion until tender. Combine the onion, corn, and spinach, mixing well. Transfer to a 1-quart baking dish. In a small bowl, combine the bread crumbs, Parmesan cheese, and margarine. Sprinkle over the vegetable mixture. Bake for 15 to 20 minutes, until the top is browned.

Makes 4 servings

Food Facts:
Spinach is a terrific source of beta-carotene and folate.

Healthier Approach:
Experiment with another leafy green - kale, also a powerhouse of nutrients.

NUTRITIONAL INFORMATION PER SERVING

Calories	157	Saturated Fat (g)	1
Protein (g)	6	Dietary Fiber (g)	4
Carbohydrate (g)	28	Sodium (mg)	483
Fat (g)	4	Cholesterol (mg)	1
Cal. from Fat (%)	23		

Triple Corn Pudding

This outstanding corn dish just means opening cans and mixes, SHHHH! It will be our secret, as this dish will quickly disappear as one of the favorites of the meal.

2 tablespoons margarine or
   butter, melted
¾ cup fat-free sour cream
1 large egg
½ cup chopped onion

1 (16¼-ounce) can corn, drained
1 (15-ounce) can cream style
   corn
1 (8½-ounce) box corn muffin
   mix

Preheat oven to 350 degrees. In a large bowl, mix together the margarine, sour cream, and egg until blended. Stir in the onion, corn, cream style corn, and muffin mix, mixing well. Pour into a 9-inch square casserole dish coated with nonstick cooking spray. Bake for 45 minutes to 1 hour or until mixture is set and light brown on top.

Makes 8 servings

Healthier Approach:
Use "no salt added" corn products.

NUTRITIONAL INFORMATION PER SERVING

Calories	270	Saturated Fat (g)	2
Protein (g)	7	Dietary Fiber (g)	4
Carbohydrate (g)	45	Sodium (mg)	712
Fat (g)	8	Cholesterol (mg)	29
Cal. from Fat (%)	25		

Wild Rice Stuffing

The wild rice combined with the tartness in the fruit and the toasty pecans make this stuffing truly extra special. If making ahead, just bake before serving. It can also be baked with whatever poultry or meat you are preparing for the occasion.

1	onion, chopped	½	teaspoon dried thyme
2	stalks celery, chopped	1	bay leaf
2	(6-ounce) boxes long grain and wild rice mix	½	cup golden raisins
		½	cup dried cranberries
4¼	cups fat-free canned chicken broth	½	cup peeled baking apples, chopped
1	teaspoon dried rosemary	⅓	cup pecan pieces, toasted

Preheat oven to 350 degrees. In a large pot coated with nonstick cooking spray, sauté the onion and celery until tender. Add wild rice with seasoning packet, chicken broth, rosemary, thyme, and bay leaf. Bring to a boil, lower heat, cover, and cook until the broth is absorbed, about 25 to 30 minutes. Stir in the raisins, cranberries, apples and pecans. Transfer the mixture to a 2-quart baking dish and bake, covered, for 20 minutes. Remove the bay leaf before serving.

Makes 6 to 8 servings

Healthier Approach:
Omit seasoning packet from rice mix and season with salt and pepper to taste. Add other dried fruit, such as dried apricots or cherries.

NUTRITIONAL INFORMATION PER SERVING

Calories	258	Saturated Fat (g)	0
Protein (g)	8	Dietary Fiber (g)	3
Carbohydrate (g)	50	Sodium (mg)	825
Fat (g)	4	Cholesterol (mg)	0
Cal. from Fat (%)	13		

Cornbread and Rice Dressing

This dressing does take a little more effort, however,
it is the ultimate dressing. Prepare the cornbread, wild rice,
and boil the eggs ahead to make putting it together quicker.
This dressing is out of this world and makes a lot!

2   (6-ounce) packages long grain
    and wild rice mix
1   (8½-ounce) box cornbread mix
4   stalks celery, chopped
2   green bell peppers, seeded
    and chopped
1   bunch green onions
    (scallions), chopped
1   onion, chopped

8   hard-boiled eggs, whites only,
    chopped
2   (8-ounce) cans mushrooms,
    stems and pieces, drained
1   (16-ounce) can fat-free
    chicken broth
1   tablespoon poultry seasoning
    Salt and pepper to taste

Preheat oven to 350 degrees. Coat a 3-quart baking dish with nonstick cooking spray. Cook the wild rice according to the package directions, omitting the margarine and salt. Prepare the cornbread according to package directions. Crumble the cornbread. In a skillet coated with nonstick cooking spray, sauté the celery, green peppers, green onions, and onion until tender. Pour into a large bowl and combine with the cooked rice, crumbled cornbread, egg whites, mushrooms, chicken broth, poultry seasoning, salt, and pepper. Place the dressing in the baking dish and bake for 45 minutes.

Makes 16 to 20 servings

NUTRITIONAL INFORMATION PER SERVING

Calories	131	Saturated Fat (g)	0
Protein (g)	5	Dietary Fiber (g)	2
Carbohydrate (g)	25	Sodium (mg)	522
Fat (g)	2	Cholesterol (mg)	0
Cal. from Fat (%)	12		

Basic Barley

Include this easy barley recipe instead of rice or pasta in your next meal. The broth makes this a tasty side; vegetable broth can be used, if desired.

4 cups water	½ cup finely chopped onion
2 teaspoons instant chicken granules	1 cup medium pearl barley
	¼ cup grated Parmesan cheese

In a pot, bring water and granules to a boil. Add onion and barley. Reduce heat, cover, and cook until barley is done, about 45 minutes to 1 hour. Toss with Parmesan cheese.

Makes 6 servings

Healthier Approach:
Add sautéed peppers, mushrooms, and tomatoes with fresh (or dried) herbs for great taste and variety.

NUTRITIONAL INFORMATION PER SERVING

Calories	143	Saturated Fat (g)	1
Protein (g)	5	Dietary Fiber (g)	5
Carbohydrate (g)	28	Sodium (mg)	81
Fat (g)	2	Cholesterol (mg)	3
Cal. from Fat (%)	10		

Barley and Mushroom Casserole

Barley is a great alternative to rice. Be creative and use whatever mushroom combinations you find in the store. Prepackaged variety dry mushrooms are available.

1 tablespoon margarine	1 cup medium barley pearl
½ pound fresh mushrooms, sliced	1 envelope onion soup mix
1 (3½-ounce) package shiitake mushrooms	4 cups water

Preheat oven to 350 degrees. In a small skillet, melt the margarine and sauté both kinds of mushrooms until tender, about 5 minutes; set aside. In a 3-quart casserole dish, combine the barley, onion soup mix, and water. Stir in the mushroom mixture. Cover with a lid and bake for 1 hour to 1 hour 15 minutes or until the barley is done and the liquid is absorbed.

Makes 6 to 8 servings

Food Facts:
Barley is a whole grain and a tasty and high fiber substitute for rice or pasta.

Healthier Approach:
Use lots of sautéed onions instead of the dry soup mix to lower salt content.

NUTRITIONAL INFORMATION PER SERVING

Calories	121	Saturated Fat (g)	0
Protein (g)	3	Dietary Fiber (g)	5
Carbohydrate (g)	23	Sodium (mg)	461
Fat (g)	2	Cholesterol (mg)	0
Cal. from Fat (%)	15		

Broccoli Casserole

My family always enjoys broccoli with cheese sauce,
yet this version is fancy enough for company. The casserole may
be refrigerated overnight. Place in a cold oven to bake and
bake for about 35 minutes or until broccoli is done.

4	(10-ounce) packages frozen broccoli spears, thawed	1	tablespoon Dijon mustard
¼	cup all-purpose flour		Salt and pepper to taste
2	cups skim milk	1	cup shredded reduced-fat sharp Cheddar cheese
1	teaspoon dry mustard	½	cup Italian bread crumbs

Preheat oven to 400 degrees. Cut about an inch off the end of the broccoli spears and discard. In a saucepan, stir together the flour and milk, stirring constantly over medium heat until the mixture comes to a boil and thickens. Whisk in the dry mustard, Dijon mustard, salt, and pepper. Remove the sauce from the heat and stir in the cheese. Place the broccoli in the bottom of a 13x9x2-inch baking dish. Spoon the cheese sauce to cover the broccoli as evenly as possible. Sprinkle bread crumbs over top of casserole. Bake for 25 minutes or until the broccoli spears are tender when pierced with the tip of a small knife.

Makes 8 servings

Food Facts:

Broccoli is not only a good source of beta carotene and Vitamin C, but also contains cancer protective "indoles." Frozen broccoli is a fine substitute for fresh. If fresh broccoli cannot be used within a few days, use frozen for best nutritional profile. Often frozen vegetables contain more nutrients since they are fresh-frozen after harvest. They may be more nutritious than a fresh vegetable that has endured transport and storage over several days.

NUTRITIONAL INFORMATION PER SERVING

Calories	131	Saturated Fat (g)	1
Protein (g)	11	Dietary Fiber (g)	5
Carbohydrate (g)	19	Sodium (mg)	297
Fat (g)	2	Cholesterol (mg)	4
Cal. from Fat (%)	14		

Broccoli and Cauliflower with Garlic Cheese Sauce

Make the sauce ahead in the day and reheat before pouring over the veggies. There's nothing boring about these veggies.

1 head cauliflower, florets only	½ cup canned fat-free chicken broth
1 bunch broccoli, florets only	
Salt and pepper to taste	1 tablespoon minced garlic
2 tablespoons all-purpose flour	½ cup shredded reduced-fat Cheddar cheese
1 cup skim milk	
	Paprika

In a large microwave covered dish, cook the cauliflower and broccoli in ½ cup water for 8 to 10 minutes or until tender. Drain any water. Salt and pepper to taste. In a small saucepan, place the flour and gradually stir in the milk and broth. Add the garlic. Cook over a medium heat until the mixture thickens, stirring constantly, about 5 minutes. Add the cheese and stir until melted. Pour over the cooked vegetables. Sprinkle with paprika and serve.

Makes 6 servings

Healthier Approach:
Some folate is lost from broccoli and cauliflower into cooking water when cooked. Save cooking water and add to soups and stews.

NUTRITIONAL INFORMATION PER SERVING

Calories	76	Saturated Fat (g)	0
Protein (g)	7	Dietary Fiber (g)	3
Carbohydrate (g)	11	Sodium (mg)	127
Fat (g)	1	Cholesterol (mg)	3
Cal. from Fat (%)	9		

Summer Squash Casserole

SIDES

Here's another way to turn squash into an incredible dish.
Make ahead and refrigerate; pop into a cold oven to bake.

2   pounds yellow squash
    (about 8), sliced
½   cup chopped onion
1   cup fat-free sour cream
Salt and pepper to taste
¼   teaspoon red pepper flakes
½   teaspoon dried basil

½   cup bread crumbs
¼   cup shredded reduced-fat
    sharp Cheddar cheese,
    optional
1   tablespoon margarine or
    butter, melted
½   teaspoon paprika

Preheat oven to 350 degrees. Coat a 1½-quart casserole dish with nonstick cooking spray. Boil the squash and onion in a saucepan in a small amount of water over medium to high heat until tender, about 5 minutes. Drain well. Combine the squash and onion with sour cream, salt, pepper, red pepper flakes, and basil in a mixing bowl. Pour into the casserole dish. Combine the bread crumbs, Cheddar cheese, margarine, and paprika. Sprinkle over the squash mixture. Bake for 20 minutes.

Makes 6 to 8 servings

Healthier Approach:
Cut the sour cream and margarine by half.

NUTRITIONAL INFORMATION PER SERVING

Calories	105	Saturated Fat (g)	1
Protein (g)	5	Dietary Fiber (g)	2
Carbohydrate (g)	16	Sodium (mg)	127
Fat (g)	2	Cholesterol (mg)	3
Cal. from Fat (%)	19		

Baked Beans

*Volunteer to prepare baked beans with
this easy recipe and you'll be the hit of the party.*

4   (15-ounce) cans white kidney
    beans (cannellini) or great
    Northern beans, rinsed and
    drained
3   whole cloves
½   small onion
1   bay leaf
½   teaspoon minced garlic

½   cup chopped onion
1   (14½-ounce) can diced
    tomatoes with juice
½   cup molasses
Dash of cayenne pepper
½   teaspoon dried thyme leaves
¼   teaspoon dried oregano
Salt and pepper to taste

Preheat oven to 350 degrees. Pour beans into a 2-quart casserole. Stick cloves into onion half and add to beans with bay leaf and garlic. In a skillet coated with nonstick cooking spray, sauté chopped onion until tender. Add to beans. Stir in tomatoes, molasses, cayenne, thyme, oregano, salt, and pepper. Cover and bake for one hour. Remove onion half and bay leaf before serving.

Makes 6 to 8 servings

Healthier Approach:
Rinse beans before adding and use "no salt added" tomatoes to lower sodium.

NUTRITIONAL INFORMATION PER SERVING

Calories	236	Saturated Fat (g)	0
Protein (g)	9	Dietary Fiber (g)	9
Carbohydrate (g)	47	Sodium (mg)	537
Fat (g)	1	Cholesterol (mg)	0
Cal. from Fat (%)	3		

Herbed Carrots

While preparing your main dish, start cooking the carrots.
This easy recipe will add color and flavor to any meal.

1 tablespoon olive oil	Black pepper to taste (freshly
1 pound fresh baby carrots	ground preferred)
¼ cup orange juice	1 teaspoon dried thyme leaves
	1 teaspoon dried rosemary

In a large skillet, heat the oil and place carrots closely together in pan in a single layer. Pour orange juice over carrots and sprinkle with ground pepper. Cover and cook over medium-low heat, turning once halfway through, for 30 minutes or until fork-tender. When carrots are tender, sprinkle with thyme and rosemary. Toss well and serve hot.

Makes 6 servings

NUTRITIONAL INFORMATION PER SERVING

Calories	53	Saturated Fat (g)	0
Protein (g)	1	Dietary Fiber (g)	1
Carbohydrate (g)	7	Sodium (mg)	27
Fat (g)	3	Cholesterol (mg)	0
Cal. from Fat (%)	43		

Artichoke and Onion Couscous

*Serve as you would rice or potatoes for
the perfect side dish to complement any meal.*

1 (10½-ounce) can beef broth
1 teaspoon olive oil
2 cups couscous
1 onion, chopped
1 teaspoon minced garlic

1 (14-ounce) can artichoke
    hearts, drained and cut in
    fourths
1 tablespoon chopped parsley
¼ cup grated Parmesan cheese

Add enough water to beef broth and oil to make 2 cups and bring to a boil.
Add couscous, stir, remove from heat and cover for 7 minutes. In a small
skillet coated with nonstick cooking spray, sauté onion and garlic until tender.
Transfer couscous to a serving dish and add onion mixture, artichoke hearts,
parsley, and cheese, tossing. Serve warm or room temperature.

Makes 8 servings

NUTRITIONAL INFORMATION PER SERVING

Calories	213	Saturated Fat (g)	1
Protein (g)	9	Dietary Fiber (g)	3
Carbohydrate (g)	39	Sodium (mg)	366
Fat (g)	2	Cholesterol (mg)	2
Cal. from Fat (%)	8		

Sautéed Mushrooms

This is fantastic served over meat to replace fattening sauces, or keep the mushrooms whole, cook them until tender, and serve as a side dish.

1 tablespoon margarine or butter

1 pound fresh mushrooms, sliced

1 green onion (scallion), sliced

½ teaspoon minced garlic

2 tablespoons Worcestershire sauce

¼ cup red wine, optional

Dash hot pepper sauce

1 teaspoon dried basil

In a skillet, melt margarine over medium heat. Add mushrooms and onions, sautéing until tender, about 5 minutes. Add the garlic, Worcestershire sauce, red wine, if using, hot sauce, and basil, cooking over low heat 5 minutes longer.

Makes 4 to 6 servings

NUTRITIONAL INFORMATION PER SERVING

Calories	42	Saturated Fat (g)	0
Protein (g)	2	Dietary Fiber (g)	1
Carbohydrate (g)	5	Sodium (mg)	85
Fat (g)	2	Cholesterol (mg)	0
Cal. from Fat (%)	42		

Spinach and Artichoke Casserole

4   (10-ounce) packages frozen
   chopped spinach, thawed
1   tablespoon margarine or
   butter
½   pound mushrooms, sliced
1½ cups fat-free sour cream
¼   cup light mayonnaise

1   (14½-ounce) can artichoke
   hearts, drained and quartered
⅓   cup grated Romano or
   Parmesan cheese
2   tomatoes, thinly sliced
¼   cup Italian bread crumbs

Preheat oven to 350 degrees. Cook spinach according to package directions; drain well. In a skillet, melt margarine and sauté mushrooms until tender. In a 2-quart casserole, combine cooked spinach, sautéed mushrooms, sour cream, mayonnaise, artichoke hearts, and cheese. Place in a 2-quart oblong casserole. Top with sliced tomatoes and sprinkle with breadcrumbs. Bake for 30 minutes or until bubbly.

Makes 8 to 10 servings

NUTRITIONAL INFORMATION PER SERVING

Calories	139	Saturated Fat (g)	1
Protein (g)	9	Dietary Fiber (g)	4
Carbohydrate (g)	17	Sodium (mg)	405
Fat (g)	5	Cholesterol (mg)	5
Cal. from Fat (%)	29		

Asparagus with Lemon Caper Vinaigrette

Attractive and amazingly wonderful. Prepare vinaigrette and prepare asparagus. Drizzle with dressing before serving.

Asparagus

1½ pounds asparagus spears (about 36), trimmed
Salt and pepper to taste

Lemon-Caper Vinaigrette (recipe follows)

Cook asparagus spears in microwave until crisp-tender. Season asparagus with salt and pepper. Place on platter and drizzle with vinaigrette.

Makes 8 servings

Lemon-Caper Vinaigrette

¼ cup fresh lemon juice
1 tablespoon olive oil
3 tablespoons capers, drained

2 tablespoons finely chopped parsley
1 teaspoon minced garlic
Black pepper to taste

Whisk together lemon juice and olive oil in a small bowl. Add capers, parsley, garlic, and pepper. May be refrigerated for one day; serve at room temperature.

Makes about ¾ cup

Food Facts:
Refrigeration helps to maintain asparagus' Vitamin C content.

NUTRITIONAL INFORMATION PER SERVING

Calories	38	Saturated Fat (g)	0
Protein (g)	2	Dietary Fiber (g)	2
Carbohydrate (g)	5	Sodium (mg)	98
Fat (g)	2	Cholesterol (mg)	0
Cal. from Fat (%)	39		

Sun-Dried Tomato Bread

This herb infused bread will have your mouth watering,
yet there's little effort involved in throwing it together.

½ cup sun-dried tomatoes	½ teaspoon dried rosemary
1¼ cups all-purpose flour	2 tablespoons chopped parsley
1 teaspoon baking powder	½ cup grated Parmesan cheese
½ teaspoon baking soda	1 large egg
1 tablespoon sugar	¾ cup skim milk
½ teaspoon minced garlic	2 tablespoons olive oil

Preheat oven to 375 degrees. Pour boiling water over tomatoes and let sit for 10 minutes. Drain water and cut into pieces; set aside. In a large bowl, combine flour, baking powder, baking soda, sugar, garlic, rosemary, parsley, and cheese. Whisk together egg, milk, and oil and stir in flour mixture until just combined. Fold in tomatoes. Transfer batter into a 7x5x3-inch loaf pan coated with nonstick cooking spray. Bake for 35 to 40 minutes.

Makes 10 servings

NUTRITIONAL INFORMATION PER SERVING

Calories	141	Saturated Fat (g)	2
Protein (g)	6	Dietary Fiber (g)	1
Carbohydrate (g)	18	Sodium (mg)	278
Fat (g)	5	Cholesterol (mg)	26
Cal. from Fat (%)	32		

Yam Biscuits

Don't fret about having to roll dough or use cookie cutters.
To make these wonderful biscuits, the dough is easy to work with
and just use a glass as your cookie cutter. Use canned yams or leftover
baked ones. For a quickie approach, use all-purpose baking
mix for the flour, omit baking powder and sugar.

3	cups all-purpose flour	2	cups cooked and mashed
5	teaspoons baking powder		sweet potatoes (yams)
2	tablespoons sugar	3	tablespoons canola oil
¼	teaspoon ground cinnamon	¾	cup skim milk

Preheat oven to 425 degrees. In a bowl, mix together flour, baking powder, sugar, and cinnamon. Make a well in the center of flour mixture. Add sweet potatoes, oil, and milk, mixing until dough is not sticky. Add additional flour if needed. Turn dough out onto a lightly floured surface and pat or roll dough to ½-inch thickness. Cut dough with a floured 2-inch biscuit cutter. Place biscuits on a baking sheet and bake for 10 to 15 minutes or until golden brown. For softer biscuits, place biscuits touching each other on baking sheet.

Makes 2 to 2½ dozen biscuits

Food Facts:
Sweet potatoes fortify these delicious biscuits with beta-carotene.

NUTRITIONAL INFORMATION PER SERVING

Calories	86	Saturated Fat (g)	0
Protein (g)	2	Dietary Fiber (g)	1
Carbohydrate (g)	16	Sodium (mg)	88
Fat (g)	2	Cholesterol (mg)	0
Cal. from Fat (%)	16		

Cornbread

This is a good basic cornbread
recipe, with the added plus of being low fat.

1　cup yellow cornmeal　　　　4　large egg whites
1　cup all-purpose flour　　　　¼　cup canola oil
1　tablespoon baking powder　1¼　cups nonfat plain yogurt
1　tablespoon sugar　　　　　¼　cup skim milk

Preheat oven to 400 degrees. Coat a 9-inch square baking pan with nonstick cooking spray. In a medium size bowl, blend the cornmeal, flour, baking powder, and sugar together. In a separate bowl, beat together the egg whites, oil, yogurt, and milk. Mix the liquids into the flour mixture until just blended. Pour the batter into the prepared baking pan. Bake for 25 minutes.

Makes 16 servings

Healthier Approach:
Try whole grain cornmeal and add ½ cup whole kernel canned corn for extra fiber and texture.

NUTRITIONAL INFORMATION PER SERVING

Calories	107	Saturated Fat (g)	0
Protein (g)	3	Dietary Fiber (g)	1
Carbohydrate (g)	15	Sodium (mg)	119
Fat (g)	4	Cholesterol (mg)	0
Cal. from Fat (%)	30		

Spinach Toast

*I love to serve this creamy spinach bread with
a bowl of hot soup. This tasty spinach mixture also makes
one of the best spinach dips! Use for parties or to introduce
spinach to your kids; they love to dip.*

2 (10-ounce) packages frozen
   chopped spinach
½ cup chopped onion
2 tablespoons all-purpose flour
1 (12-ounce) can evaporated
   skimmed milk
Salt and pepper to taste

½ teaspoon garlic powder
1 cup shredded part-skim
   mozzarella cheese
1 (16-ounce) loaf French bread,
   split in half lengthwise
Paprika

Preheat oven to 350 degrees. Prepare spinach according to the package directions; drain well. In a small saucepan coated with nonstick cooking spray, sauté the onion over medium heat 5 minutes or until tender. Add the cooked spinach and flour. Gradually stir in milk, salt, pepper and garlic powder. Cook over medium-high heat until thickened and bubbly. Remove from the heat. Add the mozzarella cheese, stirring just until mixed. Spread the spinach mixture on each cut half of the French bread. Sprinkle with the paprika. Place on a baking sheet and bake for 10 minutes or until the cheese is melted and the bread is crispy.

Makes 16 slices

NUTRITIONAL INFORMATION PER SERVING

Calories	128	Saturated Fat (g)	1
Protein (g)	7	Dietary Fiber (g)	2
Carbohydrate (g)	20	Sodium (mg)	261
Fat (g)	2	Cholesterol (mg)	5
Cal. from Fat (%)	16		

Chili Cheese Bread

*A great addition to any meal or
use with soup and/or salad for a light meal.*

1 (16-ounce) loaf French bread
1 cup shredded reduced-fat
   Cheddar cheese
1 (4-ounce) can chopped green
   chiles, drained

½ cup chopped tomato
¼ cup light mayonnaise
1 teaspoon chili powder
1 teaspoon ground cumin

Preheat oven to 350 degrees. Slice bread diagonally, slicing through but
not completely to the bottom. Combine remaining ingredients in a bowl.
Spread mixture between cut surfaces of bread. Wrap bread in foil. Bake for
20 minutes, or until cheese is melted.

Makes 16 servings

Healthier Approach:
Use whole grain or multi-grain French bread.

NUTRITIONAL INFORMATION PER SERVING

Calories	104	Saturated Fat (g)	1
Protein (g)	4	Dietary Fiber (g)	1
Carbohydrate (g)	16	Sodium (mg)	326
Fat (g)	3	Cholesterol (mg)	3
Cal. from Fat (%)	23		

Italian Puffs

BREADS

When you want an extra special bread with your meal,
make these divine rolls. They will put you in the gourmet
league, and they begin with refrigerated rolls.

1   (11.3-ounce) can refrigerated   ¼   cup sesame seeds
     whole wheat dinner rolls   ¼   cup grated Parmesan cheese
¼   cup fat-free Italian dressing

Preheat the oven to 375 degrees. Separate the rolls. In a small bowl, pour the dressing. In another small plate, combine the sesame seeds and Parmesan cheese. Dip each roll in the dressing and then roll in the sesame seed cheese mixture. Place the rolls on a baking sheet coated with nonstick cooking spray. Bake for 14 to 16 minutes or until the rolls are golden.

Makes 8 puffs

Food Facts:

These puffs are nice to accompany a salad composed of a variety of greens, chopped tomatoes, jícama, and shredded red cabbage.

NUTRITIONAL INFORMATION PER SERVING

Calories	153	Saturated Fat (g)	1
Protein (g)	6	Dietary Fiber (g)	2
Carbohydrate (g)	20	Sodium (mg)	401
Fat (g)	5	Cholesterol (mg)	2
Cal. from Fat (%)	31		

Slice and Bake Chocolate Chip Cookies

Here's a great recipe to insure hot chocolate chip cookies at a moment's notice. Store dough in the refrigerator and bake at your convenience.

½ cup margarine or butter
¾ cup dark brown sugar
⅔ cup confectioners' sugar
1 large egg
1 teaspoon vanilla extract

2¼ cups all-purpose flour
1 teaspoon baking soda
⅔ cup semisweet chocolate chips
½ cup chopped pecans, optional

In a mixing bowl, cream the margarine, brown sugar and confectioners' sugar. Add egg and vanilla, beating until fluffy. Combine flour and baking soda and add to creamed mixture. Stir in chocolate chips and pecans, if desired. Mold dough into two 12-inch logs and wrap in plastic wrap in refrigerator for 1 hour. Preheat oven to 350 degrees and cut dough into about ½-inch thick slices. Place on cookie sheet; bake for 8 minutes or until golden.

Makes 3½ dozen cookies

Healthier Approach:
Use half whole-wheat flour and add 2 to 3 tablespoons wheat germ. Toast the pecans and use less for added flavor and texture.

NUTRITIONAL INFORMATION PER COOKIE

Calories	79	Saturated Fat (g)	1
Protein (g)	1	Dietary Fiber (g)	0
Carbohydrate (g)	12	Sodium (mg)	63
Fat (g)	3	Cholesterol (mg)	5
Cal. from Fat (%)	35		

Oatmeal Crunch Cookies

*My daughter keeps a supply of these
yummy cookies in our freezer at all times to satisfy
our sweet tooth. Add chocolate chips for an extra treat.*

⅓ cup canola oil
1 cup light brown sugar
½ cup sugar
1 tablespoon vanilla extract
1 teaspoon butter extract
2 large egg whites

1½ cups all-purpose flour
½ teaspoon baking soda
½ cup natural wheat and barley
   cereal
1½ cups old-fashioned oatmeal

Preheat oven to 350 degrees. Coat a baking sheet with nonstick cooking spray.
In large bowl, stir together oil, brown sugar, and sugar. Mix in vanilla, butter
extract, and egg whites. In small bowl, mix together flour and baking soda.
Gradually stir into egg mixture. Stir in cereal and oatmeal. Drop by spoonfuls
onto baking sheet and bake for 8 to 10 minutes or until golden.

Makes 3½ to 4 dozen cookies

Food Facts:
*Adding cereal, wheat germ, or unprocessed bran for part of the flour in
cookie recipes can significantly increase the fiber content.*

NUTRITIONAL INFORMATION PER COOKIE

Calories	93	Saturated Fat (g)	0
Protein (g)	2	Dietary Fiber (g)	1
Carbohydrate (g)	16	Sodium (mg)	100
Fat (g)	2	Cholesterol (mg)	0
Cal. from Fat (%)	21		

Buttermilk Brownies

These rich brownies with a yummy icing are a chocoholic's dream. Sprinkle toasted walnuts or mix walnuts with the frosting, if desired. Cut in small squares for pick ups!

Brownies

1 cup water	½ cup buttermilk
⅓ cup canola oil	1 teaspoon baking soda
2 cups all-purpose flour	1 large egg white, well beaten
2 cups sugar	Chocolate Buttermilk Frosting
¼ cup cocoa	(recipe follows)

Preheat oven to 400 degrees. Combine water and oil in a small saucepan; bring to a boil. Combine flour, sugar, and cocoa in a mixing bowl. Add hot water mixture and stir well. Combine buttermilk and baking soda; stir until soda dissolves. Add buttermilk mixture and egg to batter; mix well. Spoon into a greased 15x10x1-inch jelly-roll pan coated with nonstick cooking spray. Bake for 15 minutes. Frost brownies with Chocolate Buttermilk Frosting while warm. Cool and cut into squares.

Makes about 3½ dozen

Chocolate Buttermilk Frosting

6 tablespoons margarine	1 (16-ounce) box confectioners'
⅓ cup buttermilk	sugar
¼ cup cocoa	½ teaspoon vanilla extract

Combine margarine, buttermilk, and cocoa in a medium saucepan; bring to a boil. Add confectioners' sugar and vanilla, blend until smooth.

Food Facts:
Buttermilk, made from nonfat milk, is low in fat - with no butter at all! By using cocoa, you are getting chocolate without the saturated fat.

NUTRITIONAL INFORMATION PER SERVING

Calories	135	Saturated Fat (g)	1
Protein (g)	2	Dietary Fiber (g)	1
Carbohydrate (g)	26	Sodium (mg)	59
Fat (g)	4	Cholesterol (mg)	0
Cal. from Fat (%)	23		

Peachy Upside Down Cake

When peach season arrives, this is always one of the first desserts I make. For an irresistible dessert, serve hot with a scoop of frozen vanilla yogurt. This cake is pretty as a picture.

4 tablespoons margarine, divided	1 teaspoon vanilla extract
¾ cup sugar, divided	1 teaspoon butter extract
1½ cups sliced, peeled ripe peaches	1 cup all-purpose flour
1 large egg	1½ teaspoons baking powder
	½ cup skim milk

Preheat oven to 350 degrees. Coat a 9-inch round cake pan with nonstick cooking spray. Melt 1 tablespoon margarine and spread in the bottom of the pan. Sprinkle with ¼ cup sugar and arrange the peaches in a circle on top, set aside. In a mixing bowl, beat together remaining 3 tablespoons margarine with ½ cup sugar. Add the egg, vanilla, and butter extract. Combine the flour and baking powder and add to the sugar mixture alternately with the milk beginning and ending with the flour. Carefully pour the batter over the peaches. Bake 30 to 35 minutes, or until a toothpick inserted comes out clean. Cool 5 minutes and invert onto a serving platter.

Makes 6 to 8 servings

Healthier Approach:
Mix blueberries or raspberries with the peaches.

NUTRITIONAL INFORMATION PER SERVING

Calories	210	Saturated Fat (g)	1
Protein (g)	3	Dietary Fiber (g)	1
Carbohydrate (g)	35	Sodium (mg)	184
Fat (g)	7	Cholesterol (mg)	27
Cal. from Fat (%)	28		

Easy Strawberry Custard Cake

By beginning with a commercially prepared pound cake,
this decadent dessert with homemade custard is simply prepared.

½ cup sugar	1 (10¾-ounce) reduced-fat frozen pound cake, thawed
¼ cup cornstarch	⅓ cup seedless raspberry jam
3 cups skim milk	1 quart strawberries
1 egg yolk, beaten	3 tablespoons orange juice
1 teaspoon vanilla extract	⅓ cup sliced almonds, toasted

In a saucepan, mix together sugar, cornstarch, and milk over medium heat, stirring until mixture comes to a boil and thickens. Add ½ cup custard mixture to yolk and return mixture to saucepan, heating well. Add vanilla; set aside to cool. Slice pound cake and place slices along bottom of a 2-quart oblong dish. Spread slices with raspberry jam. Slice strawberries and place over pound cake layer. Drizzle orange juice over berries. Carefully spread custard over strawberries. Sprinkle with toasted almonds.

Makes 10 to 12 servings

Food Facts:
Strawberries offer a high antioxidant profile, as well as a healthy dose of Vitamin C.

Healthier Approach:
Use a fat free ready-made pound cake.

NUTRITIONAL INFORMATION PER SERVING

Calories	215	Saturated Fat (g)	1
Protein (g)	3	Dietary Fiber (g)	2
Carbohydrate (g)	24	Sodium (mg)	156
Fat (g)	6	Cholesterol (mg)	19
Cal. from Fat (%)	33		

Ambrosia Crumble

For this recipe, I suggest using fresh fruit,
and for a real treat, serve over frozen vanilla yogurt. This is
one of those desserts I attack right when it comes out of the oven.

1 cup all-purpose flour	3 large navel oranges, peeled and sectioned
½ cup light brown sugar	
3 tablespoons margarine or butter	3 large bananas, sliced ½-inch thick
¼ cup flaked coconut	2 tablespoons lemon juice
2 cups fresh pineapple chunks	1 teaspoon coconut extract

Preheat the oven to 350 degrees. In a bowl, combine flour and brown sugar; cut in margarine with a pastry blender or fork until the mixture is crumbly. Set aside. In a separate bowl, combine the coconut, pineapple, oranges, bananas, lemon juice, and coconut extract; toss well. Place the fruit mixture in a 13x9x2-inch baking dish coated with nonstick cooking spray; sprinkle with the flour mixture. Bake, uncovered, for 45 minutes or until golden.

Makes 10 servings

Healthier Approach:
Try substituting whole wheat pastry flour for half of the all-purpose flour.

NUTRITIONAL INFORMATION PER SERVING

Calories	199	Saturated Fat (g)	1
Protein (g)	2	Dietary Fiber (g)	3
Carbohydrate (g)	40	Sodium (mg)	52
Fat (g)	5	Cholesterol (mg)	0
Cal. from Fat (%)	20		

Fruit Crumble

I love a crumbly topping and this is my favorite basic recipe.
I use whatever fruit is in season; however, I'm partial to blueberries.

4 cups blueberries, peeled peaches, apples or your favorite	1 teaspoon grated lemon rind
2 tablespoons sugar	⅓ cup all-purpose flour
½ teaspoon ground cinnamon, divided	⅓ cup natural wheat and barley cereal
1 tablespoon lemon juice	½ cup old-fashioned oatmeal
	¼ cup light brown sugar
	3 tablespoons margarine, melted

Preheat oven to 350 degrees. Spread fruit in a deep-dish 9-inch pie plate. Add sugar, ¼ teaspoon cinnamon, lemon juice, and lemon rind to the fruit, tossing gently to coat. In another bowl, mix together flour, cereal, oatmeal, brown sugar, and remaining ¼ teaspoon cinnamon. Stir in the melted margarine until crumbly. Sprinkle mixture over fruit. Bake for 40 to 50 minutes or until bubbly.

Makes 4 to 6 servings

Healthier Approach:
Add 1 to 2 tablespoons unprocessed bran for extra fiber.

NUTRITIONAL INFORMATION PER SERVING

Calories	229	Saturated Fat (g)	1
Protein (g)	3	Dietary Fiber (g)	4
Carbohydrate (g)	42	Sodium (mg)	128
Fat (g)	7	Cholesterol (mg)	0
Cal. from Fat (%)	25		

Blueberry Pineapple Delight

1 (20-ounce) can crushed
   pineapple in juice, undrained
2 cups fresh or frozen
   blueberries

1 (18¼-ounce) box lemon cake
   mix
⅔ cup light brown sugar
½ cup margarine or butter, melted

Preheat the oven to 350 degrees. In a 13x9x2-inch baking pan coated with nonstick cooking spray, spread the pineapple and blueberries along the bottom of the pan. Sprinkle evenly with the cake mix and brown sugar. Drizzle with the margarine. Bake for 45 to 50 minutes or until bubbly.

Makes 16 servings

Food Facts:

Blueberries are a good source of the phytochemicals, anthocyanosides, which may help prevent cancer and heart disease.

NUTRITIONAL INFORMATION PER SERVING

Calories	251	Saturated Fat (g)	2
Protein (g)	2	Dietary Fiber (g)	1
Carbohydrate (g)	39	Sodium (mg)	315
Fat (g)	10	Cholesterol (mg)	8
Cal. from Fat (%)	34		

Heavenly Yam Delight

The perfect treat to make when you are in a hurry and need a refreshing dessert. If you're a pumpkin fan, this recipe has your name on it with nutritious value. Great way to use leftover baked yams.

1 cup all-purpose flour
¼ cup plus ⅔ cup confectioners' sugar, divided
⅓ cup chopped pecans
7 tablespoons margarine or butter
1 (8-ounce) package fat-free cream cheese

1 (8-ounce) container fat-free frozen whipped topping, thawed, divided
1 (29-ounce) can sweet potatoes (yams), drained
¼ cup sugar
½ teaspoon ground cinnamon

Preheat oven to 350 degrees. In a large bowl, combine flour, ¼ cup confectioners' sugar, pecans, and margarine. Press into bottom of 13x9x2-inch baking pan. Bake 20 minutes. Set aside to cool. In a mixing bowl, mix cream cheese and remaining ⅔ cup confectioners' sugar until creamy. Fold in ¾ cup whipped topping. Spread cream cheese mixture over cooled crust. In a mixing bowl, beat sweet potatoes, sugar, and cinnamon until smooth. Spread over cream cheese mixture. Top with remaining whipped topping. Refrigerate.

Makes 16 servings

Food Facts:

Yams are a great source of beta carotene and Vitamin C. The natural sugar in yams adds to the sweetness of the dessert.

NUTRITIONAL INFORMATION PER SERVING

Calories	206	Saturated Fat (g)	1
Protein (g)	4	Dietary Fiber (g)	2
Carbohydrate (g)	32	Sodium (mg)	167
Fat (g)	7	Cholesterol (mg)	1
Cal. from Fat (%)	31		

EASY ENTERTAINING

"At a dinner party one should eat wisely but not too well, and talk well but not too wisely."

— *W. Somerset Maugham*

Super Salsa

When you need a quick recipe that makes a statement, try this salsa.

2	cups salsa	1	avocado, peeled and diced
1	(11-ounce) can Mexi-corn, drained	2	tablespoons lemon juice

In a bowl, mix together salsa, corn, avocado, and lemon juice.

Makes 3 cups, 12 (¼-cup) servings

Healthier Approach:
Use this salsa to spread on tortillas before rolling with black beans and brown rice or chicken strips.

NUTRITIONAL INFORMATION PER SERVING

Calories	62	Saturated Fat (g)	0
Protein (g)	1	Dietary Fiber (g)	2
Carbohydrate (g)	9	Sodium (mg)	334
Fat (g)	3	Cholesterol (mg)	0
Cal. from Fat (%)	38		

Black Bean and Corn Salsa

This colorful and delicious combination is a winner, with the lime juice adding that extra touch. Make the day ahead, if possible. Also makes a great salad.

1 (15-ounce) can black beans, rinsed and drained
1 (16-ounce) bag frozen corn, thawed and drained
⅓ cup chopped fresh cilantro
⅓ cup chopped green onion (scallions)
¼ cup chopped red onion

⅓ cup lime juice
1 tablespoon olive oil
2 teaspoons ground cumin
Salt and freshly ground black pepper
1½ cups chopped ripe tomatoes, drained

In a large bowl, combine beans, corn, cilantro, green onion, red onion, lime juice, oil, and cumin. Season with salt and pepper to taste. Cover and chill at least 2 hours or up to overnight. Just before serving, stir in tomatoes. Serve with chips.

Makes 4 cups, 16 (¼-cup) servings

Food Facts:
A high fiber and delicious accompaniment to fish, chicken, or homemade fajitas or burritos.

NUTRITIONAL INFORMATION PER SERVING

Calories	60	Saturated Fat (g)	0
Protein (g)	3	Dietary Fiber (g)	2
Carbohydrate (g)	11	Sodium (mg)	85
Fat (g)	1	Cholesterol (mg)	0
Cal. from Fat (%)	18		

Black-Eyed Pea Salsa

Super salsa that goes well with chips or even chicken and fish.

1 (15-ounce) can black-eyed peas, drained	1 tablespoon chopped jalapeño peppers
1 (14½-ounce) can diced tomatoes, drained	½ teaspoon ground cumin
¼ cup chopped cilantro	1 teaspoon dried oregano
1 teaspoon minced garlic	1 tablespoon red wine vinegar
1 bunch green onions (scallions), chopped	1 tablespoon olive oil
	Salt and pepper to taste

Stir together all ingredients and chill for several hours. Serve with tortilla chips.

Makes 2½ cups, 10 (¼-cup) servings

Healthier Approach:
Be sure to rinse beans to help control sodium. Also, try "no salt added" tomatoes.

NUTRITIONAL INFORMATION PER SERVING

Calories	55	Saturated Fat (g)	0
Protein (g)	3	Dietary Fiber (g)	2
Carbohydrate (g)	9	Sodium (mg)	278
Fat (g)	1	Cholesterol (mg)	0
Cal. from Fat (%)	21		

Shrimp Salsa

*This recipe takes salsa up a notch. Serve with pita chips
or crackers. Use leftover salsa with an entrée the next day.*

½ cup chopped green onions
  (scallions), diced
1 tablespoon minced garlic
1 teaspoon diced jalapeño
  peppers
2 (28-ounce) cans diced
  tomatoes, drained
⅓ cup finely chopped fresh
  cilantro

2 teaspoons dried oregano
½ teaspoon ground cumin
3 tablespoons lime juice
1 pound medium peeled shrimp,
  cooked and coarsely
  chopped
1 cup frozen corn, thawed
Salt and pepper to taste

In a bowl, combine all ingredients. Cover and chill 1 to 2 hours. Garnish with lime wedges and cilantro. Serve with chips.

Makes 6 cups, 24 (¼-cup) servings

Healthier Approach:
Serve atop fresh greens with whole grain rolls.

NUTRITIONAL INFORMATION PER SERVING

Calories	40	Saturated Fat (g)	0
Protein (g)	5	Dietary Fiber (g)	1
Carbohydrate (g)	4	Sodium (mg)	250
Fat (g)	0	Cholesterol (mg)	37
Cal. from Fat (%)	0		

Spinach Dip

This versatile dip can be used to stuff mushrooms or serve with wonton patty shells or crackers. We keep it in our refrigerator to use for snacks; just heat in microwave before serving.

1 onion, chopped
2 tablespoons all-purpose flour
1½ cups skim milk
1 cup fat-free ricotta cheese
2 (10-ounce) packages frozen
   chopped spinach, cooked
   and drained

6 ounces reduced-fat Monterey
   Jack cheese, shredded
1 (14-ounce) can artichoke
   hearts, drained and quartered
Salt and pepper to taste

In a saucepan coated with nonstick cooking spray, sauté the onion until tender. Add flour and gradually stir in milk, cooking until thickened. Add ricotta, spinach, and Monterey Jack cheese. Cook and stir until cheese is melted. Stir in artichokes and season with salt and pepper to taste.

Makes 4 cups, 64 (1-tablespoon) servings

NUTRITIONAL INFORMATION PER SERVING

Calories	16	Saturated Fat (g)	0
Protein (g)	2	Dietary Fiber (g)	0
Carbohydrate (g)	1	Sodium (mg)	49
Fat (g)	1	Cholesterol (mg)	2
Cal. from Fat (%)	28		

Strawberry Fruit Dip

Serve your favorite fruit with this sensational dip.
My girls ate the dip with a spoon.

1 quart strawberries, stemmed
   and finely chopped
¼ cup light brown sugar

¼ cup orange juice
1 cup nonfat vanilla yogurt
½ teaspoon grated orange rind

In a bowl, mix strawberries, brown sugar, orange juice, yogurt, and orange rind. Cover and chill.

Makes 2½ cups, 40 (1-tablespoon) servings

Healthier Approach:
Layer in a parfait glass with crunchy granola and sliced peaches.

NUTRITIONAL INFORMATION PER SERVING

Calories	15	Saturated Fat (g)	0
Protein (g)	0	Dietary Fiber (g)	0
Carbohydrate (g)	4	Sodium (mg)	5
Fat (g)	0	Cholesterol (mg)	0
Cal. from Fat (%)	4		

Mexican Layered Dip

This dip will be a guaranteed hit of the party. For a short cut,
use commercially prepared bean dip and avocado dip for
the layers. Serve with baked tortilla chips.

2 (15-ounce) cans black beans, rinsed and drained	1¾ cups nonfat plain yogurt, divided
3 tablespoons salsa	Salt and pepper to taste
1 cup whole kernel corn	1 (1¼-ounce) package taco seasoning mix
2 avocados, peeled and seed removed	1 bunch green onions, chopped
1 teaspoon lemon juice	1½ cups chopped tomatoes
½ teaspoon minced garlic	½ cup reduced-fat shredded Monterey Jack cheese

In a food processor, blend beans and salsa until mixture is smooth. Stir in corn. Spread mixture into a 12- to 14-inch circle on a serving platter. In another bowl, mash avocados with lemon juice and garlic. Mix in ¼ cup yogurt. Season with salt and pepper to taste. Spread on top of bean layer. In another bowl, mix remaining 1½ cups yogurt with taco seasoning mix. Spread on top of avocado mixture. Sprinkle top with green onions, tomatoes, and cheese.

Makes 25 to 30 servings

Healthier Approach:
Enjoy with sticks of carrots, crunchy jícama, or peppers, or scoop up
with cucumber wedges.

NUTRITIONAL INFORMATION PER SERVING

Calories	69	Saturated Fat (g)	1
Protein (g)	3	Dietary Fiber (g)	3
Carbohydrate (g)	9	Sodium (mg)	244
Fat (g)	3	Cholesterol (mg)	2
Cal. from Fat (%)	34		

Best Black and White Bean Spread

Serve with tortilla chips or pita and this attractive and very wonderful spread will disappear. Make ahead - great munchies.

1	(15-ounce) can white navy beans, rinsed and drained	1	(10-ounce) can chopped tomatoes and green chiles, drained	
2	tablespoons lemon juice	½	teaspoon ground cumin	
½	teaspoon minced garlic	⅓	cup picante sauce or salsa	
2	tablespoons grated Parmesan cheese	1	tomato, chopped	
1	(15-ounce) can black beans, drained and rinsed	½	cup chopped green onions (scallions)	
		½	cup shredded reduced-fat Cheddar cheese	

In a food processor, combine navy beans, lemon juice, garlic, and Parmesan cheese; process until smooth. Spread white bean mixture on half of a round serving platter. In food processor, combine black beans, tomatoes and green chiles, and cumin, process until smooth. Spread on remaining half of serving platter. Cover with salsa and sprinkle with tomato, green onion, and cheese.

Makes 12 to 16 servings

Food Facts:
Beans are a great source of protein and this spread provides a delicious way to get it.

Healthier Approach:
Be sure to rinse beans to keep sodium in check.

NUTRITIONAL INFORMATION PER SERVING

Calories	68	Saturated Fat (g)	0
Protein (g)	5	Dietary Fiber (g)	3
Carbohydrate (g)	11	Sodium (mg)	332
Fat (g)	1	Cholesterol (mg)	1
Cal. from Fat (%)	11		

Tropical Fruity Cheese Spread

You can whip this spread together quickly. It's a wonderful combination of flavors that will quickly attract a crowd. Serve with crackers or sweet crackers, such as gingersnaps.

3 (8-ounce) packages fat-free cream cheese
1 (4-ounce) package blue cheese, crumbled
1 cup shredded reduced-fat Cheddar cheese
1 cup chopped dates
¼ cup chopped pecans, toasted

Combine all ingredients except pecans. Shape into a round mold on a plate. Cover and chill. Top with pecans before serving.

Makes 4 cups, 32 (2-tablespoon) servings

Healthier Approach:
Try adding bits of chopped dried apricots, cherries, figs, and cranberries, too, if desired.

NUTRITIONAL INFORMATION PER SERVING

Calories	61	Saturated Fat (g)	1
Protein (g)	5	Dietary Fiber (g)	0
Carbohydrate (g)	6	Sodium (mg)	187
Fat (g)	2	Cholesterol (mg)	5
Cal. from Fat (%)	32		

Crab and Avocado Mold

*An attractive and delicious mold that combines
two favorites - guacamole and seafood. Serve with crackers.
Make ahead and unmold the day of serving.*

First Layer

1½ packages unflavored gelatin
½ cup boiling water
2 (8-ounce) containers
   guacamole dip

1 teaspoon hot sauce
1 teaspoon Worcestershire
   sauce
Second layer (recipe follows)

Dissolve gelatin in boiling water. Add guacamole, hot sauce, and Worcester-shire sauce. Transfer into a round mold coated with nonstick cooking spray and refrigerate. Allow to set and top with second layer.

Second Layer

1½ packages unflavored gelatin
½ cup boiling water
½ cup evaporated skimmed milk
2 tablespoons lemon juice
2 (8-ounce) packages fat-free
   cream cheese
Salt and pepper to taste

⅓ cup light mayonnaise
1 teaspoon hot sauce
1 pound lump crabmeat or
   shrimp
¼ cup chopped onion
1 bunch green onions
   (scallions), chopped

Dissolve gelatin in boiling water. In a separate bowl, mix evaporated milk, lemon juice, cream cheese, salt, pepper, mayonnaise, and hot sauce. Fold in crabmeat. Combine gelatin and milk mixtures; add onion and green onions. Pour this layer on top of first guacamole layer that has set. Refrigerate until set. To serve, invert mold onto a serving platter.

Makes 30 servings

Food Facts:
Although avocado, the basic ingredient of guacamole, is high in fat, it is mostly monounsaturated. Researchers have found that these fats may help protect health.

NUTRITIONAL INFORMATION PER SERVING

Calories	65	Saturated Fat (g)	1
Protein (g)	7	Dietary Fiber (g)	0
Carbohydrate (g)	3	Sodium (mg)	196
Fat (g)	3	Cholesterol (mg)	26
Cal. from Fat (%)	43		

Chicken Rosemary Strips

A great item for the buffet table. Make ahead and reheat for the party. Your family will also enjoy this as a dinner entrée.

½ cup fat-free Italian dressing
¼ cup lemon juice
1 tablespoon minced garlic
2 tablespoons Worcestershire sauce

1 tablespoon dried rosemary
Black pepper to taste
2 pounds boneless skinless chicken breasts, cut into strips

In a bowl, mix Italian dressing, lemon juice, garlic, Worcestershire sauce, rosemary, and pepper. Pour over chicken strips and marinate for at least 30 minutes or overnight. Place strips on a broiler pan and pour marinade on top. Broil 10 minutes on each side or until done. Baste while cooking with marinade.

Makes 12 to 16 serving

Healthier Approach:
Serve with grilled or roasted vegetables - also great on the buffet table, and can be served cold.

NUTRITIONAL INFORMATION PER SERVING

Calories	69	Saturated Fat (g)	0
Protein (g)	13	Dietary Fiber (g)	0
Carbohydrate (g)	2	Sodium (mg)	130
Fat (g)	1	Cholesterol (mg)	33
Cal. from Fat (%)	10		

Marinated Shrimp

Wonderful, fantastic! I used the leftovers the next day
and made a salad - just tossed the shrimp and sauce with lettuce.

½ teaspoon minced garlic	½ teaspoon hot sauce
⅓ cup sliced green onions (scallions)	1 tablespoon capers, drained
½ cup chopped red bell pepper, optional	1 tablespoon prepared horseradish
2 tablespoons olive oil	2 teaspoons Dijon mustard
3 tablespoons lemon juice	2 pounds cooked medium shrimp, peeled

In a large bowl, combine all ingredients except shrimp. Add shrimp; tossing to coat. Cover and refrigerate 4 to 6 hours or overnight. Remove to serving bowl and serve with toothpicks.

Makes 30 to 40 shrimp, depending on size

Healthier Approach:
Try adding different veggies with the shrimp to marinate and serve. Just cut in chunks the right size for serving with toothpicks.

NUTRITIONAL INFORMATION PER SERVING

Calories	31	Saturated Fat (g)	0
Protein (g)	5	Dietary Fiber (g)	0
Carbohydrate (g)	0	Sodium (mg)	65
Fat (g)	1	Cholesterol (mg)	44
Cal. from Fat (%)	29		

Seafood Toast

*These simple to prepare, incredible appetizers can be
made ahead and frozen. If freezing, spread seafood mixture on
bread, freeze in single layers and when frozen, store in zip-lock bags.
Add topping consisting of sour cream and cheese before baking.*

5 ounces fat-free cream cheese, softened
2 tablespoons margarine, softened
1 (4-ounce) can chopped green chiles, drained
1 (4¼-ounce) can small shrimp, drained
1 (4¼-ounce) can crabmeat, drained

Several dashes of hot pepper sauce
1 cup shredded reduced-fat sharp Cheddar cheese, divided
36 slices cocktail bread (honey grain wheat)
⅔ cup fat-free sour cream
Dash of salt, if desired
Paprika

Preheat oven to 350 degrees. In a bowl, blend together the cream cheese and margarine. Stir in green chiles, shrimp, crabmeat, hot pepper sauce, and ½ cup cheese. Spread on top of the cocktail bread. In another bowl, mix together the sour cream, remaining ½ cup cheese, and salt. Top each prepared bread slice with a dollop of sour cream mixture. Sprinkle with paprika. Bake for 15 minutes. Serve.

Makes 36 toasts

Healthier Approach:
Add finely chopped onion, celery, and green and red pepper to cheese mixture.

NUTRITIONAL INFORMATION PER SERVING

Calories	65	Saturated Fat (g)	0
Protein (g)	5	Dietary Fiber (g)	1
Carbohydrate (g)	9	Sodium (mg)	214
Fat (g)	2	Cholesterol (mg)	10
Cal. from Fat (%)	20		

Roasted Red Pepper and Mushroom Polenta Pizza

This no trouble fabulous dish is made with roasted peppers in a jar. If desired, purchase already prepared polenta instead of making the crust.

1⅓ cups ground cornmeal
1 cup all-purpose flour
¼ teaspoon salt
¾ cup warm water
2 tablespoons olive oil
1 tablespoon dried basil
¼ cup grated Parmesan cheese

¾ cup fat-free ricotta cheese
1 teaspoon minced garlic
1 cup shredded part-skim mozzarella cheese
1 cup sliced mushrooms
1 (7-ounce) jar roasted red peppers, drained

Preheat oven to 425 degrees. In a bowl, combine cornmeal, flour, and salt. Combine water and olive oil and mix with cornmeal mixture, stirring until dry ingredients are moistened. Press into bottom of a 13x9x2-inch pan coated with nonstick cooking spray. Bake for 5 minutes. Meanwhile, in a bowl, mix together basil, Parmesan, ricotta, garlic, and mozzarella. Spread over partially baked crust. Top with mushrooms and red peppers. Return to oven and bake for 30 minutes or until crust is set and top is bubbly.

Makes 35 squares

Food Facts:
Polenta is made from cornmeal simmered in water. After it is cooled, it is sliced and can be served with a variety of toppings.

NUTRITIONAL INFORMATION PER SERVING

Calories	53	Saturated Fat (g)	1
Protein (g)	2	Dietary Fiber (g)	1
Carbohydrate (g)	7	Sodium (mg)	108
Fat (g)	2	Cholesterol (mg)	2
Cal. from Fat (%)	29		

Glazed Pork Roast with Maple-Mustard Sauce

This sweetly glazed pork is a welcome change for any buffet.
Prepare roast ahead, and then preslice, reassemble,
and serve with this incredible sauce.

Roast

1 (4-pound) boneless loin pork roast, or 2 (1-pound) pork tenderloins	2 tablespoons Dijon mustard
	2 tablespoons dry mustard
	1 teaspoon black pepper
½ cup finely chopped onion	Maple Mustard sauce
1 cup maple syrup	(recipe follows)
¼ cup cider or cane vinegar	

Trim roast of any excess fat; set aside. In a small bowl, whisk onion, syrup, vinegar, Dijon and dry mustards, and pepper in a medium saucepan. Place the pan over moderately high heat and boil, stirring occasionally until the mixture is reduced to 1¾ cups, about 20 minutes. Preheat the oven to 425 degrees. Brush the glaze over the entire roast. Place the roast on a rack in a shallow pan lined with foil. Roast for 30 minutes, brushing with the glaze every 15 minutes. Reduce the oven temperature to 375 degrees. Bake for 35 to 45 more minutes, or until a meat thermometer inserted in the middle of the roast reads 170 degrees. Brush the roast with glaze every 10 minutes, using about half the glaze. Remove the roast from the oven and cool to room temperature. Wrap it in foil and refrigerate until it is well chilled. Serve with Maple Mustard Sauce and bread slices.

Makes 16 servings on buffet

Maple-Mustard Sauce

1 (12-ounce) can evaporated skimmed milk	½ cup maple syrup
	Salt and pepper to taste
3 tablespoons dry mustard	¼ cup cider vinegar
1 tablespoon all-purpose flour	2 tablespoons Dijon mustard

In a small pot, mix together milk, dry mustard, flour, syrup, salt, pepper, vinegar, and Dijon. Cook over moderate heat, whisking constantly until the mixture comes to a full boil and thickens. Boil for 1 minute, whisking constantly. Remove from heat, place in a bowl, and cover with plastic wrap directly on the mustard. The mustard sauce may be refrigerated, covered, for several weeks. Stir before using. Serve at room temperature.

Glazed Pork Roast *continued*

Food Facts:
Dry mustard can be found in your spice section of the grocery store.

NUTRITIONAL INFORMATION PER SERVING

Calories	188	Saturated Fat (g)	1
Protein (g)	15	Dietary Fiber (g)	0
Carbohydrate (g)	25	Sodium (mg)	151
Fat (g)	3	Cholesterol (mg)	38
Cal. from Fat (%)	16		

Chili Boats

*This great and easy recipe is perfect party food
as you can make it at your leisure and store in the freezer
until ready to use. They also make great snacks.*

2 (12-ounce) packages soft   2 cups shredded reduced-fat
   party rolls (20 to a package)   Cheddar cheese
1 (15-ounce) can turkey chili
   without beans

Preheat oven to 350 degrees. Split the rolls in half. Indent bottom of each roll with fingertips. Put a small amount of chili (about 1 teaspoon) and a little shredded cheese on bottom half of roll. Replace top. Store in refrigerator or freeze until ready to use. Bake for 15 minutes or until cheese is melted.

Makes 40 chili boats

Healthier Approach:
Use meatless chili.

NUTRITIONAL INFORMATION PER SERVING

Calories	71	Saturated Fat (g)	1
Protein (g)	4	Dietary Fiber (g)	1
Carbohydrate (g)	9	Sodium (mg)	112
Fat (g)	2	Cholesterol (mg)	4
Cal. from Fat (%)	23		

Italian Pizza Slices

*These wonderful pizza slices make the perfect
pick up when company is coming or they can be used as
the bread of the evening for that extra touch.*

1 (16-ounce) loaf French bread, cut into 12 to 14 slices	1 cup chopped Roma tomatoes or tomatoes
1 tablespoon olive oil	Salt and pepper to taste
2 tablespoons minced garlic	1 teaspoon dried basil
½ cup chopped green onions (scallions)	1 tablespoon lemon juice
	¼ cup grated Parmesan cheese

Preheat the broiler. Arrange the slices of bread on a baking sheet, cut-side up, and broil until lightly browned. Turn slices to other side and broil. Watch carefully. In a skillet coated with nonstick cooking spray, heat the olive oil and sauté the garlic, green onions, tomatoes, salt, pepper, and basil for several minutes. Add the lemon juice. Spoon the mixture evenly on top of the bread slices and sprinkle with the Parmesan cheese. Return to broiler and broil just until the cheese melts, about 2 minutes, watch carefully.

Makes 12 to 14 slices

Healthier Approach:
Can be prepared with whole wheat French bread; add extra finely chopped vegetables, such as green and red peppers.

NUTRITIONAL INFORMATION PER SERVING

Calories	114	Saturated Fat (g)	1
Protein (g)	4	Dietary Fiber (g)	1
Carbohydrate (g)	19	Sodium (mg)	233
Fat (g)	3	Cholesterol (mg)	1
Cal. from Fat (%)	20		

Cranberry and White Chocolate Chip Cookies

*The sweet white chocolate combined with the tartness of cranberries
makes this a fantastic cookie and perfect for the holidays!*

½ cup margarine, softened	1⅓ cups old-fashioned oatmeal
⅔ cup sugar	1 teaspoon baking soda
1 large egg, slightly beaten	1 cup dried cranberries
½ teaspoon ground cinnamon	½ cup white chocolate chips
1¾ cups all-purpose flour	

Preheat oven to 350 degrees. In a large bowl, beat together margarine, sugar, and egg until smooth and creamy. In a separate bowl, mix together the cinnamon, flour, oatmeal, and baking soda until well combined. Gradually add the dry mixture to the margarine mixture. Stir in the dried cranberries and white chocolate chips, stirring to blend. Drop dough by rounded teaspoons onto a cookie sheet coated with a nonstick cooking spray; bake for 10 to 12 minutes.

Makes 3 dozen cookies

Healthier Approach:
This recipe can be prepared with additional finely chopped fruit. Chips can be omitted.

NUTRITIONAL INFORMATION PER COOKIE

Calories	95	Saturated Fat (g)	1
Protein (g)	1	Dietary Fiber (g)	1
Carbohydrate (g)	14	Sodium (mg)	73
Fat (g)	4	Cholesterol (mg)	6
Cal. from Fat (%)	35		

Cranberry and White Chocolate Treats

The tartness of cranberries combined with crunchy ingredients makes this recipe the ideal pick up treat. Keep these ingredients in your pantry to prepare when you're in a pinch.

1⅓ cups graham cracker crumbs
2 tablespoons sugar
5 tablespoons margarine or butter, melted
1 cup dried cranberries
⅓ cup white chocolate chips

⅓ cup chopped walnuts
½ cup natural wheat and barley cereal
1 (14-ounce) can fat-free sweetened condensed milk

Preheat oven to 350 degrees. In a 13x9x2-inch baking pan, mix graham cracker crumbs, sugar, and margarine; press along bottom of pan. Sprinkle cranberries, white chocolate chips, walnuts, and cereal evenly over graham cracker crust. Pour sweetened condensed milk over top. Bake for 25 minutes or until bubbly.

Makes 4 dozen squares

Food Facts:
Walnuts might be high in fat, but 70% of the fat is polyunsaturated.

Healthier Approach:
Add additional dried fruit of choice with cranberries.

NUTRITIONAL INFORMATION PER SERVING

Calories	70	Saturated Fat (g)	1
Protein (g)	1	Dietary Fiber (g)	0
Carbohydrate (g)	11	Sodium (mg)	48
Fat (g)	2	Cholesterol (mg)	1
Cal. from Fat (%)	31		

Pistachio Marble Cake

*How can such a simple cake be so wonderful
a presentation and so delicious to eat? I keep these
ingredients in my pantry for that emergency dessert.*

1 (18¼-ounce) package
 reduced-fat yellow cake mix
1 large egg
3 large egg whites
¼ cup canola oil
1 (4-serving) package pistachio
 instant pudding mlx

¼ cup skim milk
1 cup fat-free sour cream
¼ cup chopped pecans
½ cup semisweet chocolate
 chips
⅔ cup chocolate syrup

Preheat oven to 325 degrees. In a mixing bowl beat cake mix, egg, egg whites, and oil together. Add pudding mix, milk, and sour cream to batter and beat for several minutes until creamy. Coat a bundt pan with nonstick cooking spray and sprinkle with nuts and chocolate chips. Carefully pour three-fourths of the batter into pan. Add chocolate syrup to remaining batter and drop by tablespoons on top batter in pan. Using a knife, marble the chocolate. Bake for 50 to 60 minutes or until a toothpick inserted in the middle comes out clean. Cool in pan 20 minutes and invert onto a serving plate.

Makes 16 servings

Healthier Approach:
A good way to cut fat in any recipe that calls for chocolate chips is to switch to mini-chocolate chips and use half the amount called for. Because they are so small, they distribute well in the product and fool the taste buds into thinking there's more.

NUTRITIONAL INFORMATION PER SERVING

Calories	265	Saturated Fat (g)	2
Protein (g)	4	Dietary Fiber (g)	1
Carbohydrate (g)	46	Sodium (mg)	332
Fat (g)	8	Cholesterol (mg)	15
Cal. from Fat (%)	25		

White Chocolate Bundt Cake with Raspberry Sauce

Keep these ingredients in your pantry to whip up this incredible cake in a pinch. This cake is great with or without the sauce, and will be the star whenever it is made.

Cake

1 (18¼-ounce) box reduced-fat yellow cake mix
1 (4-serving) box instant white chocolate pudding and pie filling
1 cup fat-free sour cream
¼ cup canola oil
⅔ cup skim milk
1 large egg
3 large egg whites
½ cup white chocolate chips
½ cup chopped pecans
1½ cups confectioners' sugar
¼ cup skim milk
1 tablespoon almond extract
Raspberry Sauce (recipe follows)

Preheat oven to 350 degrees. Coat a 10-inch bundt pan with nonstick cooking spray. In a mixing bowl, combine cake mix, pudding, sour cream, oil, milk, egg, and egg whites, blending until well mixed. Stir in white chocolate chips and pecans. Pour into bundt pan and bake for 40 to 50 minutes or until wooden pick inserted comes out clean. Meanwhile, in a small bowl, mix confectioners' sugar, milk, and almond extract; set aside. Cool cake on rack for 10 minutes before inverting on serving plate. Drizzle glaze over warm cake. Serve with Raspberry Sauce.

Makes 16 servings

Raspberry Sauce

2 (10-ounce) packages frozen raspberries in syrup, thawed, divided
¼ cup sugar
2-3 tablespoons orange juice or orange liqueur

Drain 1 package raspberries and discard juice. Save juice from other package. Purée fruit, juice, sugar, and orange juice in a food processor or blender; strain purée to remove seeds, if desired. Chill until ready to use.

Makes 1½ cups sauce

Food Facts:
White chocolate is essentially sweetened cocoa butter, and is slightly higher in fat, calories, and cholesterol than semisweet chocolate.

Healthier Approach:
Any fruit sauce could be used, including strawberry, blueberry, mango, or a mixture.

NUTRITIONAL INFORMATION PER SERVING

Calories	330	Saturated Fat (g)	2
Protein (g)	5	Dietary Fiber (g)	2
Carbohydrate (g)	60	Sodium (mg)	337
Fat (g)	9	Cholesterol (mg)	16
Cal. from Fat (%)	23		

Cranberry Orange Bundt Cake

A perfect holiday cake, however, I keep cranberries in the freezer to enjoy this recipe year round. Dried cranberries also work great.

3	cups all-purpose flour	1	tablespoon grated orange rind
1½	teaspoons baking soda	1½	cups buttermilk
½	cup canola oil	2	cups finely chopped fresh or frozen cranberries
1¼	cups sugar		
1	large egg	½	cup confectioners' sugar
3	large egg whites	2	tablespoons orange juice

Preheat oven to 350 degrees. Combine flour and soda; set aside. In a mixing bowl, beat oil and sugar until creamy. Add egg, egg whites, and orange rind; beat mixture until light and fluffy. Add the dry ingredients alternately with the buttermilk ending with dry ingredients just until blended. Stir in cranberries. Pour batter into a 10-inch bundt pan coated with nonstick cooking spray. Bake 45 to 50 minutes or until cake tests done when a toothpick inserted into the cake comes out clean. Cool 10 minutes in pan. Remove from pan and invert on serving plate. Mix together confectioners' sugar and orange juice; drizzle over cake.

Makes 24 servings

Healthier Approach:
Serve with orange slices, if desired. (The orange slices are especially good with just a tad of cocoa powder sprinkled on top.)

NUTRITIONAL INFORMATION PER SERVING

Calories	161	Saturated Fat (g)	1
Protein (g)	3	Dietary Fiber (g)	1
Carbohydrate (g)	26	Sodium (mg)	105
Fat (g)	5	Cholesterol (mg)	9
Cal. from Fat (%)	28		

Yam Cranberry Bundt Cake

A perfect holiday cake with the spices,
sweetness of yams, and tartness of cranberries. I enjoy this
cake better than fruitcakes and it makes a great holiday gift.

⅔ cup margarine
1 cup sugar
1 large egg
3 large egg whites
2 (15-ounce) cans sweet
   potatoes (yams), drained and
   mashed (2 cups)
3 cups all-purpose flour
1 teaspoon ground cinnamon
½ teaspoon ground nutmeg

1 teaspoon baking powder
1 teaspoon baking soda
1 teaspoon vanilla extract
1 cup coarsely chopped
   cranberries
½ cup chopped walnuts, optional
2 tablespoons flaked coconut
1 tablespoon orange juice
1 cup confectioners' sugar

Preheat oven to 350 degrees. In a mixing bowl, beat together margarine and sugar until blended. Add egg and egg whites, one at a time, beating well after each addition. Mix in sweet potato. In another bowl, mix together flour, cinnamon, nutmeg, baking powder, and baking soda. Gradually add flour mixture to creamed mixture, beating well after each addition. Add vanilla and cranberries. Pour half of batter into a 10-inch bundt pan coated with nonstick cooking spray. Sprinkle walnuts and coconut over batter. Cover with remaining batter. Bake about 50 minutes or until a wooden pick inserted in center of cake comes out clean. Cool in pan on a wire rack for 10 minutes; invert onto a serving plate. In small bowl, mix together orange juice and confectioners' sugar. Spoon glaze over cake.

Makes 16 servings

Food Facts:
This dessert has been supplemented with the beta carotene in sweet potatoes - no need for guilt.

NUTRITIONAL INFORMATION PER SERVING

Calories	293	Saturated Fat (g)	2
Protein (g)	5	Dietary Fiber (g)	2
Carbohydrate (g)	50	Sodium (mg)	265
Fat (g)	8	Cholesterol (mg)	13
Cal. from Fat (%)	26		

Ultimate Coconut Cake

By starting with a cake mix, this amazing cake really isn't much trouble. The homemade custard between the layers iced with the cream cheese icing makes every bite melt in your mouth.

Cake

1 (18¼-ounce) box reduced-fat yellow cake mix
1 teaspoon coconut extract

Custard Filling (recipe follows)
Cream Cheese Icing
  (recipe follows)

Preheat oven to 350 degrees. Prepare cake mix according to package directions adding coconut extract. Bake in three 9-inch round pans coated with nonstick cooking spray. Bake 15 to 20 minutes or until a toothpick inserted in cake comes out clean. Cool. Spread custard filling between layers and frost sides and top with Cream Cheese Icing. Refrigerate.

Makes 16 servings

Custard Filling

1   cup sugar
3   tablespoons cornstarch
1   cup skim milk

⅓   cup flaked coconut
1   teaspoon vanilla extract

Mix sugar with cornstarch in a saucepan. Gradually add milk and cook over medium heat until mixture begins to thicken. Add coconut and continue to cook until thick. Stir in vanilla; cool slightly. Spread between layers.

Cream Cheese Icing

6   ounces reduced fat cream cheese
2   tablespoons margarine or
    butter

3   cups confectioners' sugar
1   teaspoon coconut extract

In a mixing bowl, mix together the cream cheese and margarine. Gradually add the confectioner' sugar. Add coconut extract. Frost cake and refrigerate.

Healthier Approach:
Top with your favorite tropical fruit, such as mango slices, kiwi, or pineapple chunks.

NUTRITIONAL INFORMATION PER SERVING

Calories	297	Saturated Fat (g)	2
Protein (g)	3	Dietary Fiber (g)	0
Carbohydrate (g)	62	Sodium (mg)	269
Fat (g)	5	Cholesterol (mg)	6
Cal. from Fat (%)	14		

Ultimate Cheesecake

There's nothing better than a slice of good cheesecake and here's a #1 recipe. Serve with fresh fruit topping or a fruit sauce for a memorable dessert. Freezes well.

1 cup graham cracker crumbs	1 cup sugar
1 tablespoon sugar	2 large eggs
1 teaspoon grated lemon rind	3 large egg whites
1 tablespoon margarine, melted	3 tablespoons all-purpose flour
2 (8-ounce) packages fat-free cream cheese	1 teaspoon vanilla extract
1 (15-ounce) container light ricotta cheese	2 cups fresh fruit such as strawberries, blueberries, or kiwi
1 cup plain nonfat yogurt	

Preheat oven to 325 degrees. In the bottom of a 9-inch springform pan, mix together the graham cracker crumbs, sugar, lemon rind, and melted margarine. Press mixture along the bottom and sides of pan. In a mixing bowl beat together the cream cheese, ricotta, yogurt, and sugar until smooth. Gradually add eggs and egg whites, beating well. Add the flour and vanilla. Pour into the crust and bake for one hour. Turn oven off and leave in oven with door ajar for one hour. Refrigerate cheesecake until well chilled. Serve with fresh fruit.

Makes 12 servings

Healthier Approach:
This recipe can be prepared crustless, if desired.

NUTRITIONAL INFORMATION PER SERVING

Calories	245	Saturated Fat (g)	3
Protein (g)	13	Dietary Fiber (g)	1
Carbohydrate (g)	35	Sodium (mg)	360
Fat (g)	6	Cholesterol (mg)	50
Cal. from Fat (%)	23		

Sweet Potato Pecan Pie

I'm a pecan pie lover and here's the ultimate combo.
A favorite of mine all year round. Try using the homemade
pie crust on page 213 for a homemade healthier crust.

1 refrigerated 9-inch pie crust	¼ teaspoon nutmeg
1 (15-ounce) can yams (sweet potatoes) drained and mashed (1 cup)	3 large egg whites
	⅔ cup dark corn syrup
	½ cup sugar
2 large eggs, divided	2 teaspoons vanilla extract
¼ cup light brown sugar	⅔ cup pecans, chopped
½ teaspoon cinnamon	

Preheat oven to 350 degrees. Lay pie crust in a 9-inch pie dish. In a mixing bowl, blend together the yams, 1 egg, brown sugar, cinnamon, and nutmeg. Spread evenly in bottom of pie crust. In a mixing bowl, beat together the remaining egg, egg whites, corn syrup, sugar, and vanilla until mixture is frothy. Stir in pecans. Carefully spoon over yam layer. Bake for 50 to 60 minutes or until filling is set around edges or until a knife inserted halfway between the center and edge comes out clean. Cool and serve.

Makes 8 servings

Healthier Approach:
Use a reduced-fat graham cracker crust; decrease pecans to ⅓ cup. Enjoy a small serving (divide the pie into 10 servings)! Use pie crust recipe in this section.

NUTRITIONAL INFORMATION PER SERVING

Calories	397	Saturated Fat (g)	2
Protein (g)	6	Dietary Fiber (g)	2
Carbohydrate (g)	65	Sodium (mg)	267
Fat (g)	14	Cholesterol (mg)	53
Cal. from Fat (%)	31		

Banana Pie with Chocolate Glaze

*Banana pudding fans will love this fabulous pie.
I needed a quick dessert and looked around my house
for a solution that would appeal to all.*

Crust

2   cups finely crushed reduced-
    fat vanilla wafers
2   tablespoons margarine or
    butter, melted

1   teaspoon vanilla extract
2-3 bananas, sliced
Custard (recipe follows)
Glaze (recipe follows)

Preheat oven to 375 degrees. In a 9-inch pie plate, mix vanilla wafers, margarine, and vanilla together and pat into the pie plate. Bake for 5 to 7 minutes or until golden brown. Cool and arrange banana slices on top of crust. Top with Custard and Glaze.

Custard

3   tablespoons cornstarch
¾   cup sugar
1½ cups skim milk

1   large egg, slightly beaten
1   teaspoon butter extract

In a medium saucepan, mix together the cornstarch and sugar. Gradually add the milk and heat, stirring constantly until mixture comes to a boil. Gradually add about ¾ cup hot custard to egg, stirring, and then transfer mixture back to pot; continue cooking for one minute. Remove from heat; add extract and spoon custard over top of bananas.

Glaze

1   tablespoon cocoa
1   tablespoon margarine or
    butter, melted

3   tablespoons confectioners'
    sugar
1   tablespoon hot water, if needed

In a small bowl mix cocoa, margarine, and confectioners' sugar. Gradually add water to make a thick glaze consistency. Pour glaze on top to cover. Refrigerate for several hours.

Makes 8 servings

Food Facts:

In order for a product to be labeled "reduced-fat", it must contain 25% less fat than the original product. It does not necessarily mean "low fat"!

Banana Pie *continued*

Healthier Approach:
Try phyllo sheets (4 or 5) sprayed with cooking spray as an alternative to this or just about any pie crust.

NUTRITIONAL INFORMATION PER SERVING

Calories	325	Saturated Fat (g)	1
Protein (g)	4	Dietary Fiber (g)	2
Carbohydrate (g)	63	Sodium (mg)	90
Fat (g)	7	Cholesterol (mg)	27
Cal. from Fat (%)	20		

Pie Crust

Here's a great pie crust to use when you want a healthier approach to your favorite pie. The recipe is not time consuming and makes a tasty crust!

1 **cup all-purpose flour**
½ **cup natural wheat and barley cereal**
¼ **cup canola oil**
4 **tablespoons ice water**

In a food processor or mixing bowl, mix together flour and cereal. Add oil, stirring until mixed. Gradually add water, mixing until dough sticks together to form a ball. Refrigerate dough for 1 hour, if time permits. On a lightly floured surface, roll out dough into a ¼-inch thick circle to fit into a pie plate. Transfer to pie plate. Preheat oven to 350 degrees. Bake crust for 30 to 35 minutes or until done. If filling pie, follow directions of the pie recipe.

Makes 8 servings

Food Facts:
This pie crust recipe is far healthier with regard to fat than a prepared crust made with hydrogenated fat or lard.

NUTRITIONAL INFORMATION PER SERVING

Calories	141	Saturated Fat (g)	1
Protein (g)	2	Dietary Fiber (g)	1
Carbohydrate (g)	18	Sodium (mg)	48
Fat (g)	7	Cholesterol (mg)	0
Cal. from Fat (%)	44		

Banana Pudding Trifle

This is banana pudding taken to the most incredible level.
Great presentation and outstanding dessert! Don't let a trifle
intimidate you - it is just a layering of ingredients. For extra pizzazz,
drizzle banana liqueur over vanilla wafers when layering.

⅔ cup sugar	6 bananas, divided
¾ cup all-purpose flour	2 (1.4-ounce) English toffee
3½ cups skim milk	candy bars, crushed, divided
2 large egg yolks, slightly beaten	1 (8-ounce) container fat-free
1 tablespoon vanilla extract	frozen whipped topping,
1 (11-ounce) box reduced-fat	thawed
vanilla wafers, divided	

In a large saucepan, combine the sugar and flour. Gradually stir in the milk and bring the mixture to a boil over a medium-high heat, stirring constantly. Place the egg yolks in a small bowl and gradually pour some of the hot custard into the egg yolks, mixing well with a fork. Gradually, pour the hot custard mixture back into the saucepan with the remaining custard, cooking over a low heat for several minutes. Do not boil. Remove from the heat and add the vanilla. Transfer the custard to a bowl and allow to cool (can refrigerate to speed up the cooling). In a trifle bowl or large glass bowl, place one-third of the vanilla wafers. Slice 2 of the bananas and place on top the wafers. Spread one-half of the custard on top and sprinkle with one-half of the crushed candy bars. Repeat the layers again using all of the remaining custard and crushed candy bars. Place the final one-third layer of the vanilla wafers on top. Add 2 sliced bananas and top with the whipped topping.

Makes 16 servings

NUTRITIONAL INFORMATION PER SERVING

Calories	252	Saturated Fat (g)	1
Protein (g)	4	Dietary Fiber (g)	1
Carbohydrate (g)	49	Sodium (mg)	43
Fat (g)	4	Cholesterol (mg)	30
Cal. from Fat (%)	15		

FREEZER FRIENDLY FOODS

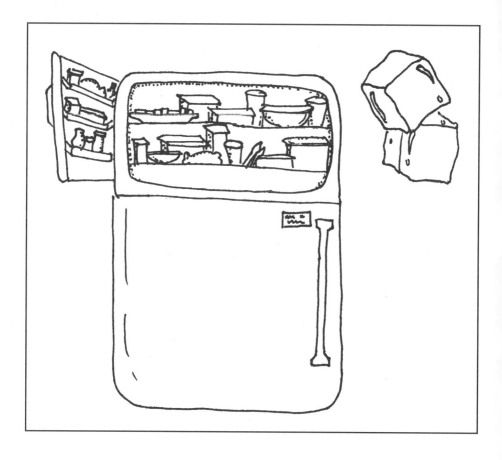

M. O. M.

Manager of Other People's Messes

Corn and Wild Rice Soup

This hearty soup is full of great taste and textures, making it a meal to remember. Perfect for winter months or the holiday time of year.

1	(6-ounce) package long grain and wild rice mix	3	tablespoons all-purpose flour
2	pounds frozen corn, thawed	1	onion, chopped
2	(14½-ounce) cans fat-free chicken broth, divided	½	cup finely diced carrots
		1½	cups skim milk
			Salt and pepper to taste

Prepare the wild rice according to the package directions, omitting any oil and salt; set aside. Meanwhile, combine the corn, 1 can chicken broth, and flour in a food processor until the mixture is puréed or the corn is thickened and creamy; set aside. In a large pot coated with nonstick cooking spray, sauté the onion and carrots cooking until the vegetables are tender, about 5 minutes. Add the corn mixture, wild rice, and the remaining can of chicken broth. Cook for 10 minutes or until very well heated. Add the milk and continue cooking until hot. Season to taste.

Makes 8 servings

Healthier Approach:
Add additional chopped vegetables, if desired.

NUTRITIONAL INFORMATION PER SERVING

Calories	212	Saturated Fat (g)	0
Protein (g)	10	Dietary Fiber (g)	4
Carbohydrate (g)	45	Sodium (mg)	471
Fat (g)	1	Cholesterol (mg)	1
Cal. from Fat (%)	3		

Black Bean Chili

I made this recipe for a luncheon and everyone wanted the recipe. The squash and corn enhanced the chili with flavor and color. Serve over rice, if desired.

2	cups dried black beans, rinsed	6	cups water
1	cup chopped red onion	1	(10½-ounce) can diced
1	cup diced carrot		tomatoes and green chiles
½	cup chopped red bell pepper		Salt and pepper to taste
½	cup chopped green bell pepper	1	cup diced zucchini
1	tablespoon minced garlic	1	cup diced yellow squash
2	tablespoons chili powder	1	cup frozen corn
2	teaspoons ground cumin	1	tablespoon seeded and finely
½	teaspoon cayenne pepper		chopped jalapeño peppers
1	bay leaf		

Place the beans in a large bowl and cover with cold water. Let stand at least 4 hours or overnight. Drain. In a large pot coated with nonstick cooking spray, sauté the onion, about 5 minutes. Add the carrot, peppers, garlic, chili powder, cumin, cayenne, and bay leaf. Continue cooking, stirring often, until the vegetables are tender, about 10 minutes. Add the black beans and the 6 cups of water. Bring to a boil, reduce heat, cover and simmer 1 hour. Add the tomatoes and chiles, salt, and pepper and continue cooking, uncovered, until the beans are tender and the mixture is thick, 45 to 60 minutes. Add the zucchini, yellow squash, corn and jalapeños, cooking until the vegetables are tender, about 10 minutes.

Makes 8 servings

Note: If in a pinch, you can reduce the soaking time for the beans by placing them in water three times their amount. Bring to a boil and boil, uncovered, for 2 minutes. Remove from the heat, cover and let sit for 1 hour. Drain, rinse and use as directed in the recipe. To make the quick version, just substitute canned black beans!

Food Facts:
High in fiber. Serve over brown rice, if desired.

NUTRITIONAL INFORMATION PER SERVING

Calories	215	Saturated Fat (g)	0
Protein (g)	13	Dietary Fiber (g)	13
Carbohydrate (g)	41	Sodium (mg)	177
Fat (g)	1	Cholesterol (mg)	0
Cal. from Fat (%)	5		

Wonderful White Chili with Tomato Salsa

Outstanding selection! I had to have seconds of this one. Leftover chicken and canned chicken broth can be used to make this chili when you're in a hurry. A dollop of the Tomato Salsa and a sprinkle of reduced-fat Cheddar cheese will knock the chili up a notch.

Chili

1½ pounds boneless skinless chicken breasts, cut into pieces
1 onion, quartered
8 cups water
1 onion, chopped
1 teaspoon minced garlic
2 (15½-ounce) cans great Northern beans, rinsed and drained, divided

4 cups chicken broth, reserved from cooking the chicken, divided
1 teaspoon chili powder
1 teaspoon ground cumin
½ teaspoon dried oregano
1 (4-ounce) can diced green chiles, drained
1 (14½-ounce) can white sweet corn, drained
Tomato Salsa (recipe follows), optional

In a large pot, place the chicken pieces and the quartered onion. Cover with 8 cups of water and bring to a boil. Cook at a low boil for 20 to 30 minutes or until the chicken is tender. Reserve the broth, and cut the chicken into bite-size pieces. Discard the onion. In a large pot coated with nonstick cooking spray, sauté the chopped onion and garlic over a medium-high heat for 3 to 5 minutes or until tender, stirring constantly. In a food processor, place 1 can great Northern beans with 1 cup of the chicken broth and process until smooth. Add the smooth bean mixture, remaining can great Northern beans, remaining 3 cups chicken broth, chili powder, cumin, oregano, green chiles, and corn to the pot with onion. Bring to a boil, reduce heat and cook for 20 to 30 minutes. Serve with a dollop of Tomato Salsa.

Makes 6 to 8 servings

Tomato Salsa

1½ cups chopped tomato
2 tablespoons chopped fresh cilantro

½ teaspoon minced garlic
¼ cup chopped red onion
½ teaspoon sugar

In a bowl, mix together the tomato, cilantro, garlic, red onion and sugar. Cover and refrigerate until ready to use.

Healthier Approach:
Omit chicken for a vegetarian chili. Add a variety of other beans (pinto beans, black beans, garbanzo beans, etc.)

NUTRITIONAL INFORMATION PER SERVING

Calories	209	Saturated Fat (g)	0
Protein (g)	27	Dietary Fiber (g)	7
Carbohydrate (g)	28	Sodium (mg)	786
Fat (g)	1	Cholesterol (mg)	49
Cal. from Fat (%)	5		

Southwestern Soup

*This wonderful, hearty soup has a
little of everything and pleases families.*

1	pound ground sirloin	3	cups cubed peeled potatoes
1	cup chopped onion	½	teaspoon chili powder
2	cups water	1	teaspoon ground cumin
1	(10-ounce) can diced	½	teaspoon minced garlic
	tomatoes and green chiles		Salt and pepper to taste
	with their juice	2	cups frozen corn
1	cup salsa		

In a large pot over a medium-high heat, cook the sirloin and onion until the sirloin is done, about 5 to 7 minutes; drain any excess grease. Add the water, tomato and green chiles, salsa, potatoes, chili powder, cumin, garlic, salt, and pepper. Bring to a boil. Reduce heat, cover, and simmer for about 30 minutes. Add the corn and continue cooking, covered, for 15 minutes longer. Cool and freeze in containers.

Makes 8 to 10 servings (10 cups)

Healthier Approach:
Delete meat and substitute 1 can black beans for a wonderful, filling soup.

NUTRITIONAL INFORMATION PER SERVING

Calories	180	Saturated Fat (g)	2
Protein (g)	12	Dietary Fiber (g)	3
Carbohydrate (g)	20	Sodium (mg)	252
Fat (g)	7	Cholesterol (mg)	29
Cal. from Fat (%)	32		

Spinach Lasagne

With spinach and red sauce, you won't miss the meat
in this scrumptious dish. No need to bake before freezing.

1 cup chopped onion
½ pound mushrooms, sliced
1 teaspoon minced garlic
1 (15-ounce) can tomato sauce
1 (14½-ounce) can Italian-style tomatoes, drained and chopped
Salt and pepper to taste
1 teaspoon dried basil
1 teaspoon dried oregano
1 bay leaf

1 (8-ounce) package lasagna noodles
2 (10-ounce) packages frozen chopped spinach, thawed and drained
2 cups part-skim ricotta cheese
1 large egg white, slightly beaten
1 (8-ounce) package shredded reduced-fat Monterey Jack cheese

Preheat oven to 350 degrees. In a large saucepan over medium-high heat, sauté the onion, mushrooms, and garlic until tender, about 5 minutes. Add the tomato sauce, tomatoes, salt, pepper, basil, oregano, and bay leaf. Bring to a boil. Cover, reduce heat, and simmer for 5 minutes, stirring occasionally. Remove the bay leaf, and set the tomato mixture aside. Cook the lasagna noodles according to the package directions omitting oil and salt. Drain well; set aside. Combine the spinach, ricotta cheese, and egg white, mixing well; set aside. Spread one-third of the reserved tomato mixture in the bottom of a 13x9x2-inch baking pan coated with nonstick cooking spray. Layer half of the lasagna noodles and then half of the spinach mixture. Top with one-third of the tomato mixture and half of the cheese. Top with the remaining lasagna noodles, spinach mixture, tomato mixture and cheese in that order. Cover and bake for 40 minutes; uncover and bake an additional 10 minutes.

Makes 8 servings

Healthier Approach:
Try using kale instead of spinach for a change.

NUTRITIONAL INFORMATION PER SERVING

Calories	321	Saturated Fat (g)	7
Protein (g)	24	Dietary Fiber (g)	5
Carbohydrate (g)	34	Sodium (mg)	372
Fat (g)	11	Cholesterol (mg)	39
Cal. from Fat (%)	30		

Salsa Lasagne

This great vegetarian variation of a traditional lasagne is made with
no fuss. Bake before freezing or boil noodles and freeze uncooked.

1 (10-ounce) can diced tomatoes and green chiles with juice	1 (8-ounce) package lasagna noodles, uncooked
1 (16-ounce) jar thick and chunky salsa	1 (16-ounce) container fat-free cottage cheese
1 (8-ounce) can tomato sauce	2 large egg whites
1 tablespoon dried oregano	1 (8-ounce) package shredded part-skim mozzarella cheese
Black pepper to taste	1 (15-ounce) can black beans, drained and rinsed

Preheat the oven to 350 degrees. Coat a 2-quart oblong baking dish with nonstick cooking spray. Combine the tomatoes, salsa, tomato sauce, oregano and pepper in a large bowl; set aside. Spread a heaping cup of the tomato mixture in the bottom of the pan. Top with four of the lasagna noodles. In a food processor, blend the cottage cheese and egg whites until smooth. Top with half the cottage cheese mixture, half the mozzarella, half the black beans and four more lasagna noodles. Continue layering and top with the remaining tomato mixture. Cover tightly with foil; place additional foil underneath the pan (it may bubble over). Bake for 1 hour to 1 hour, 15 minutes or until the noodles are tender.

Makes 8 to 10 servings

Food Facts:
Both salsa and tomatoes provide lycopene, a potentially cancer preventive
substance that is especially available in cooked tomato products.

Healthier Approach:
To lower sodium, use "no salt added" tomato products.

NUTRITIONAL INFORMATION PER SERVING

Calories	222	Saturated Fat (g)	2
Protein (g)	17	Dietary Fiber (g)	4
Carbohydrate (g)	29	Sodium (mg)	857
Fat (g)	4	Cholesterol (mg)	17
Cal. from Fat (%)	18		

Cheese Stuffed Manicotti

Manicotti filled with cheese is a great standby for a luncheon or a light dinner. No need to bake before freezing.

Manicotti

1 cup chopped onion	1 (10¾-ounce) can tomato purée
½ cup chopped green bell pepper	1 teaspoon dried oregano
½ cup shredded carrots	1 teaspoon dried basil
½ pound mushrooms, sliced	½ teaspoon sugar
½ cup sliced celery	Salt and pepper to taste
½ cup water	12 manicotti shells
1 teaspoon minced garlic	Cheese Filling (recipe follows)
1 (14½-ounce) can chopped tomatoes, with their juice	

Preheat oven to 350 degrees. In a medium saucepan, combine onion, green pepper, carrots, mushrooms, celery, water, and garlic, cooking until the vegetables are tender, about 7 minutes. Stir in the tomatoes, tomato purée, oregano, basil, sugar, salt, and pepper. Bring to a boil. Reduce heat, cover, and simmer for 15 minutes, stirring occasionally. Meanwhile, cook the manicotti shells according to the package directions omitting any oil and salt. Drain well. Fill each manicotti shell with about ⅓ cup of the Cheese Filling. Arrange the filled shells in a 3-quart rectangular baking dish coated with nonstick cooking spray. Pour the sauce over the filled shells. Bake for 35 to 40 minutes or until heated through.

Makes 6 servings

Cheese Filling

2 large egg whites, beaten	2 tablespoons chopped parsley
1 (15-ounce) container part-skim ricotta cheese	½ teaspoon dried basil
	½ teaspoon dried oregano
1 cup shredded part-skim mozzarella cheese	Salt and pepper to taste

In a mixing bowl, stir together the egg whites, ricotta cheese, mozzarella cheese, parsley, basil, oregano, salt, and pepper.

Food Facts:
Homemade pasta sauce is truly a treat. But if you are short on time, use a low-fat bottled red sauce.

Healthier Approach:
Use fat-free ricotta cheese.

NUTRITIONAL INFORMATION PER SERVING

Calories	336	Saturated Fat (g)	6
Protein (g)	21	Dietary Fiber (g)	4
Carbohydrate (g)	43	Sodium (mg)	236
Fat (g)	10	Cholesterol (mg)	33
Cal. from Fat (%)	25		

Ultimate Red Pasta Sauce

This rich, flavorful sauce is a sneaky way of getting veggies in your diet. Throw in your favorite veggies; chop them very finely in the food processor. Serve over large pasta shells for a change. The sauce even tastes better after freezing.

1	medium onion, chopped	½	cup water or chicken broth
½	cup chopped celery	1	tablespoon dried oregano
½	cup finely chopped carrots	1	bay leaf
1	teaspoon minced garlic	1	teaspoon dried basil
1	(28-ounce) can puréed tomatoes	2	tablespoons chopped parsley
			Pinch of sugar
1	(6-ounce) can tomato paste		Salt and pepper to taste

In a large pan coated with nonstick cooking spray, sauté the onion, celery, carrots, and garlic over medium high for 5 minutes. Add the tomatoes, tomato paste, water, oregano, bay leaf, basil, parsley, sugar, salt, and pepper. Cook over a medium heat for another 15 minutes. Remove bay leaf before serving. Serve over pasta of your choice.

Makes 6 servings

Healthier Approach:
Add finely diced leftover vegetables, such as peppers, mushrooms, and summer squash.

NUTRITIONAL INFORMATION PER SERVING

Calories	93	Saturated Fat (g)	0
Protein (g)	4	Dietary Fiber (g)	4
Carbohydrate (g)	21	Sodium (mg)	558
Fat (g)	0	Cholesterol (mg)	0
Cal. from Fat (%)	2		

Chicken Enchilada Casserole

A great dish to pull out of the freezer as it melts in your mouth with each bite. No need to bake before freezing.

½ cup chopped onion
1 tablespoon minced garlic
1 (14½-ounce) can diced tomatoes, drained
½ cup thinly sliced green onions (scallions), divided
1 (4-ounce) can chopped green chiles, drained
3 cups cooked chicken breasts chunks
⅓ cup all-purpose flour
1 (12-ounce) can evaporated skimmed milk
½ cup canned fat-free chicken broth
½ teaspoon chili powder
½ teaspoon ground cumin
6 (6-inch) flour tortillas, quartered
1 cup shredded reduced-fat Monterey Jack cheese
1 cup shredded reduced-fat Cheddar cheese

Preheat oven to 350 degrees. In a skillet coated with nonstick cooking spray, sauté onion and garlic until tender. Add tomatoes and bring to a boil. Reduce heat and cook for 10 minutes. Add ¼ cup green onions, green chiles, and chicken, stirring until mixed. In a saucepan, place flour and gradually add milk. Heat over medium heat, whisking constantly, until mixture is thickened and bubbly. Add broth, chili powder, and cumin. In a 2½-quart round dish, spread ½ cup sauce. Layer tortillas, chicken mixture, sauce, and cheeses. Repeat layers twice. Bake for 40 minutes or until heated thoroughly. Sprinkle with remaining green onions before serving.

Makes 8 servings

Healthier Approach:
Try whole wheat tortillas.

NUTRITIONAL INFORMATION PER SERVING

Calories	347	Saturated Fat (g)	4
Protein (g)	31	Dietary Fiber (g)	2
Carbohydrate (g)	31	Sodium (mg)	701
Fat (g)	10	Cholesterol (mg)	59
Cal. from Fat (%)	26		

Chicken Vermicelli

*A great family dinner. The recipe serves many so I always
put one casserole in the freezer to take to someone's home when food
is needed. The vermicelli can be cooked in water or reserved broth.*

2½ pounds boneless skinless chicken breasts
2 large green bell peppers, seeded and chopped, divided
2 onions, chopped, divided
Salt and pepper to taste
1 (16-ounce) package vermicelli
1 tablespoon minced garlic
1 (10-ounce) can diced tomatoes and green chiles
2 tablespoons Worcestershire sauce
1½ cups shredded reduced-fat sharp Cheddar cheese
1 (17-ounce) can green peas, drained
1 (8-ounce) can mushroom stems and pieces, drained

In a large pot, add the chicken, 1 green pepper, and 1 onion. Cover with water and boil until the chicken is done, about 20 to 30 minutes. Remove the chicken from the stock and chop into bite-size pieces. Strain the broth to remove the onion and green pepper. Cook the vermicelli in the chicken broth, and drain, saving the broth to add as needed. In a large skillet coated with nonstick cooking spray, sauté the remaining green pepper, remaining onion, and garlic. Add the tomatoes, Worcestershire sauce, and cheese, cooking until the cheese is melted. Stir in the peas and mushrooms. Add the chicken and vermicelli, stirring to mix well and heat through. Add more broth to thin out the sauce if necessary. Serve or transfer to a casserole for serving later. To reheat, bake at 350 degrees for 30 minutes or until bubbly.

Makes 16 servings

Healthier Approach:
Try serving this recipe with spaghetti squash instead of vermicelli. Ask for spaghetti squash in your produce department if you are unfamiliar with it.

NUTRITIONAL INFORMATION PER SERVING

Calories	246	Saturated Fat (g)	1
Protein (g)	25	Dietary Fiber (g)	4
Carbohydrate (g)	31	Sodium (mg)	341
Fat (g)	2	Cholesterol (mg)	43
Cal. from Fat (%)	9		

Mexican Lasagne

Combine Southwestern flavor with lasagne and
you have an instant success. No need to cook before freezing.

1 pound ground sirloin
⅔ cup chopped onion
1 (14½-ounce) can chopped tomatoes, with juice
2 (8-ounce) cans tomato sauce
1 tablespoon dried oregano
¼ teaspoon crushed red pepper flakes
2 tablespoons chili powder
1 (15-ounce) can pinto beans, rinsed and drained

1 (8-ounce) package lasagna noodles
1 cup reduced-fat ricotta cheese
1 large egg white
2 tablespoons chopped green chiles
1 (8-ounce) package reduced-fat Monterey Jack cheese, shredded

Preheat the oven to 375 degrees. In a large skillet, sauté the sirloin and onion until meat is done, about 7 minutes; drain any excess grease. Add the tomatoes, tomato sauce, oregano, red pepper, and chili powder. Add the pinto beans and simmer, uncovered, 15 minutes. Meanwhile, cook the noodles according to package directions, omitting any salt and oil. In a small bowl, combine the ricotta cheese, egg white and green chiles; set aside. Spread 1 cup of the meat sauce over the bottom of a 13x9x2-inch casserole dish coated with nonstick cooking spray. Top with half the noodles, overlapping slightly. Sprinkle with half the remaining meat sauce. Spoon all of the ricotta cheese mixture over the meat mixture and spread it out lightly. Top with half the shredded cheese, the remaining noodles, and the remaining meat sauce and cheese. Bake, covered with foil, for 30 to 40 minutes. Uncover and bake 10 minutes more or until bubbly.

Makes 10 to 12 servings

Healthier Approach:
Add another can of pinto beans, or a combination of pinto and black beans, and delete meat.

NUTRITIONAL INFORMATION PER SERVING

Calories	282	Saturated Fat (g)	5
Protein (g)	22	Dietary Fiber (g)	4
Carbohydrate (g)	24	Sodium (mg)	574
Fat (g)	11	Cholesterol (mg)	44
Cal. from Fat (%)	35		

Shrimp Casserole

A great standby for a shrimp and rice casserole.
Freeze before cooking.

MAIN DISH MEALS

1½ pounds medium shrimp, peeled
½ green bell pepper, seeded and chopped
½ cup chopped onion
1 teaspoon minced garlic
3 tablespoons all-purpose flour
1½ cups skim milk

1½ cups cooked rice
1 tablespoon lemon juice
Salt and pepper to taste
½ cup soft bread crumbs
1 tablespoon grated Parmesan cheese
1 tablespoon chopped parsley

Preheat the oven to 350 degrees. In a large skillet coated with nonstick cooking spray, over medium-high heat, cook the shrimp, pepper, onion, and garlic, about 5 minutes, until the vegetables are tender and the shrimp are pink. Gradually stir in the flour and milk. Cook 5 minutes or until the mixture is thickened and bubbly, stirring constantly. Stir in cooked rice, lemon juice, salt, and pepper. Remove from the heat and pour into a 2-quart casserole dish coated with nonstick cooking spray. In a small bowl, combine the bread crumbs, cheese and parsley. Sprinkle over the shrimp mixture. Bake for 15 minutes or until thoroughly heated.

Makes 4 to 6 servings

Healthier Approach:
Try this recipe with brown rice. Add additional chopped vegetables, such as chopped broccoli, red peppers, and summer squash.

NUTRITIONAL INFORMATION PER SERVING

Calories	262	Saturated Fat (g)	1
Protein (g)	29	Dietary Fiber (g)	1
Carbohydrate (g)	28	Sodium (mg)	290
Fat (g)	3	Cholesterol (mg)	174
Cal. from Fat (%)	11		

Shrimp Fettuccine

The cheesy sauce makes this fettuccine dish a real winner.
Use any type of pasta. No need to bake before freezing.

1   (16-ounce) package fettuccine
2   pounds medium shrimp, peeled
1   large onion, chopped
1   green bell pepper, seeded and
     chopped
⅓   cup chopped parsley
½   pound mushrooms, sliced
1   teaspoon minced garlic

⅓   cup all-purpose flour
1   (12-ounce) can evaporated
     skimmed milk
1   (8-ounce) package reduced-fat
     sharp Cheddar cheese,
     shredded
1   bunch green onions
     (scallions), sliced

Preheat the oven to 350 degrees. Cook the fettuccine according to package directions, omitting any oil and salt. Drain and set aside. Meanwhile, in a large pot coated with nonstick cooking spray, sauté the shrimp, onion, green pepper, parsley, mushrooms, and garlic over medium heat until tender, about 5 minutes. Mix in the flour. Gradually add the evaporated milk, stirring until thickened. Add the cheese and green onions, stirring until the cheese is melted and shrimp is done. Toss with the pasta. Transfer to a casserole dish and bake for 20 minutes.

Makes 8 to 10 servings

Healthier Approach:
Add chopped red bell pepper and broccoli, if desired.

NUTRITIONAL INFORMATION PER SERVING

Calories	320	Saturated Fat (g)	1
Protein (g)	33	Dietary Fiber (g)	2
Carbohydrate (g)	38	Sodium (mg)	398
Fat (g)	4	Cholesterol (mg)	144
Cal. from Fat (%)	12		

Orange Raspberry Ice Cream Dessert

The most refreshing summer dessert.

2   (3-ounce) packages lady
    fingers, split
2   quarts fat-free vanilla frozen
    yogurt or ice cream,
    softened, divided
1   (6-ounce) can frozen orange
    juice
1   (12-ounce) package frozen
    raspberries

1   (11-ounce) can mandarin
    oranges, drained
1   (8-ounce) can crushed
    pineapple, drained
1   tablespoon frozen lemonade
    concentrate
1   teaspoon almond extract

Line bottom and sides of a 9-inch springform pan with ladyfingers. In a bowl, mix 1 quart softened ice cream with orange juice. Pour into pan and freeze until firm. Place raspberries, oranges, pineapple, and lemonade in a food processor or blender, blending until smooth. Spoon over firm orange layer and refreeze. Add almond extract to remaining ice cream and spoon over raspberry layer. Freeze several hours or overnight.

Makes 12 to 16 servings

Healthier Approach:
Top with fresh whole strawberries, raspberries, or fresh pineapple chunks.

NUTRITIONAL INFORMATION PER SERVING

Calories	191	Saturated Fat (g)	0
Protein (g)	7	Dietary Fiber (g)	1
Carbohydrate (g)	39	Sodium (mg)	81
Fat (g)	1	Cholesterol (mg)	40
Cal. from Fat (%)	5		

Lemon Cheesecake with Raspberry Sauce

*Attention cheesecake and lemon lovers: here is
the ultimate dessert. Serve with Raspberry Sauce and you'll
always make room for dessert. Freezes well; defrost before serving.*

Cheesecake

1   cup gingersnap cookie crumbs
2   tablespoons margarine or
    butter, melted
3   (8-ounce) packages fat-free
    cream cheese
1   cup sugar
2   large eggs

2   large egg whites
3   tablespoons all-purpose flour
1   tablespoon grated lemon rind
1   (8-ounce) container nonfat
    lemon yogurt
1   teaspoon vanilla extract
Raspberry Sauce (recipe follows)

Preheat oven to 350 degrees. To make crust, mix together gingersnap crumbs
and margarine and pat along bottom of a 9-inch springform pan coated with
nonstick cooking spray. In a mixing bowl, beat together the cream cheese and
sugar until smooth. Add the eggs and egg whites, one at a time, beating until
creamy. Add the flour, lemon rind, yogurt, and vanilla. Pour cheese mixture
into prepared crust. Bake for 50 to 60 minutes or until center is set. Turn oven
off, cool cheesecake in oven. Cover and chill 6 to 8 hours. Remove sides of
springform pan. Serve with Raspberry Sauce.

Makes 12 servings

Raspberry Sauce

1   (12 ounce) package frozen
    sweetened raspberries,
    thawed (about 2 cups)

2   tablespoons lemon juice
1½ tablespoons cornstarch

Combine all ingredients in saucepan; bring to a boil. Cook over medium-high
heat, stirring until thickened. Remove from heat, cover and chill. If raspberries
are unsweetened, add about ⅓ cup sugar.

Makes 1¼ cups sauce

Healthier Approach:
Try with a variety of sliced fresh or frozen fruit.

Lemon Cheesecake *continued*

NUTRITIONAL INFORMATION PER SERVING

Calories	238	Saturated Fat (g)	1
Protein (g)	12	Dietary Fiber (g)	1
Carbohydrate (g)	39	Sodium (mg)	413
Fat (g)	4	Cholesterol (mg)	40
Cal. from Fat (%)	16		

Lemon Ice

*This incredible, luscious lemon ice will
not be limited to only lemon lovers. For another
serving idea, freeze in a bowl and scoop out in balls.*

2 **cups evaporated skimmed
milk**
1 **cup sugar**

2 **tablespoons grated lemon rind**
⅓ **cup lemon juice (fresh
preferred)**

In a bowl, combine together the evaporated skimmed milk, sugar, lemon rind, and lemon juice, stirring until well mixed. Pour into an 8-inch square pan. Freeze until firm.

Makes 8 servings

Healthier Approach:
Serve as an accompaniment to a bowl of fresh blueberries. Garnish with mint leaves.

NUTRITIONAL INFORMATION PER SERVING

Calories	149	Saturated Fat (g)	0
Protein (g)	5	Dietary Fiber (g)	0
Carbohydrate (g)	33	Sodium (mg)	74
Fat (g)	0	Cholesterol (mg)	2
Cal. from Fat (%)	0		

Banana Split Pie

A dessert that appeals to kids, adults, or company. Use your favorite flavored frozen yogurt to create your own fabulous frozen wonder.

1½ cups chocolate wafer crumbs	3 bananas, mashed
¼ cup sugar	2 tablespoons cocoa
3 tablespoons margarine, melted, divided	⅔ cup confectioners' sugar
	2 tablespoons hot water
3 teaspoons vanilla extract, divided	1 cup raspberries, strawberries, or seasonal fruit
½ gallon nonfat frozen vanilla yogurt, softened	

Preheat oven to 375 degrees. In an oblong 3-quart glass dish (13x9x2-inch), mix together chocolate crumbs, sugar, 2 tablespoons margarine, and 1 teaspoon vanilla. Pat into the bottom of the dish. Bake for 10 minutes. Cool completely. In a large bowl, mix together the yogurt, bananas, and 1 teaspoon vanilla. Quickly spread on top of cooled crust. Place in the freezer until the yogurt layer is set. In a small bowl, mix together the remaining 1 tablespoon margarine, cocoa, confectioners' sugar, remaining 1 teaspoon vanilla, and hot water, stirring until smooth. Remove partially frozen dessert from freezer and quickly drizzle with chocolate sauce. Return to freezer for several hours or overnight. Top with fresh seasonal fruit.

Healthier Approach:
Adding fresh fruit to any dessert is a fine way to add freshness, good taste, and redeeming nutritional quality.

Makes 16 servings

NUTRITIONAL INFORMATION PER SERVING

Calories	212	Saturated Fat (g)	1
Protein (g)	6	Dietary Fiber (g)	2
Carbohydrate (g)	40	Sodium (mg)	93
Fat (g)	4	Cholesterol (mg)	2
Cal. from Fat (%)	16		

"By the time you look for a good parking place at the grocery store, you can already be off the produce aisle. Anyway, we need the exercise!"

— *Courtney Clegg*

Tips and Tricks

- Freeze recipes in zip-top bags to store easily in freezer.

- If using salt in cooking, don't salt water until after it comes to a boil. Salted water has a higher boiling point, therefore, salted water takes longer to boil.

- When boiling pasta or rice, add a bouillon cube or broth for more flavor.

- Asparagus stems will break off at the appropriate point if you hold the stalk with both hands and bend.

- For a speedy answer to cutting up veggies, raid the salad bar.

- To de-seed cucumbers, cut in half and run the pointed end of a teaspoon down the center, scooping the seeds out.

- Use a microwave for thawing foods quickly or for melting or softening margarine.

- When broiling, line bottom of pan with foil to make clean up easier.

- When polishing silver, try using ketchup, as the acidity of the tomatoes will actually clean your silver.

- To keep fruit rinds from getting stuck in the grater when grating, cover grater with plastic wrap. (Or buy the dried version in the spice section.)

- To prevent egg shells from cracking, add a pinch of salt to the water before hard boiling.

- To get the most juice out of fresh lemons, bring them to room temperature or warm them slightly and roll them under your palm against the kitchen counter before squeezing.

- When a cake recipe calls for flouring the baking pan, use a little of the dry cake mix instead...no white covering on outside of cake.

- Oops...For a quickie remedy if you over-salt a dish while it's cooking, drop in a peeled and cut raw potato, as it will absorb the excess salt; remove potato before serving.

- If you have over-sweetened a dish, add salt.

- Place a slice of apple or a slice of soft bread in a container of hardened brown sugar to soften it back up.

- If time permits, the best method of removing excess fat from recipes is refrigeration until the fat hardens. Put a piece of wax paper over the top of soup, etc. - it can be peeled right off, along with the hardened fat.

Stock Your Pantry with Cooking Staples:

Refrigerator Staples

Cheese (varieties of reduced fat)

Eggs

Fruit

Onion

Garlic

Green onion

Lemon Juice

Mixed greens

Margarine or butter

Skim milk

Sour cream (fat free)

Tomato

Unprocessed bran

Wheat germ

Yogurt (plain fat free)

Pantry Staples

Barley

Bread (whole wheat or white)

Bread crumbs (Italian or plain)

Broth (canned, cubes, or granules)

Bulgur (yes, try using it)

Canned beans (variety)

Couscous

Evaporated skimmed milk

Green chilies (diced)

Olive oil

Pasta (assorted shapes and flavors)

Quinoa (yes, try this, too)

Rice (wild, brown, and white)

Salt

Diced tomatoes and green chilies (canned)

Canned tomatoes (diced, sauce)

Tomato paste and sauce

Baking Staples

Baking powder

Baking soda

Semi-sweet chocolate chips

Canola oil

Cocoa

Cornstarch

Dried fruit

Flour (all-purpose and whole wheat)

Natural wheat and barley cereal

Nonstick cooking spray

Oatmeal

Sugar (granulated, brown, and confectioners')

Extracts (vanilla, almond, butter, and coconut)

Condiment Staples

Capers
Hot sauce
Honey
Ketchup

Mayonnaise (low fat or fat free)
Mustard
Pasta sauces
Salad dressings (fat free or reduced fat)

Salsa
Soy sauce (reduced sodium)
Vinegar (balsamic, cider, or distilled)
Worcestershire sauce

Spice Pantry Staples

Basil leaves
Bay leaves
Chili powder
Cinnamon (ground)
Cumin (ground)
Curry
Dill weed

Garlic powder
Ginger (ground)
Nutmeg
Oregano
Paprika
Parsley flakes

Pepper (black, coarsely ground)
Red pepper flakes
Rosemary
Tarragon leaves
Thyme leaves

Frozen Pantry Staples

Chicken breasts
Fish
Frozen veggies (spinach, corn…)

Pork tenders
Shrimp
Sirloin (ground or roast)

Turkey breast (whole or ground)
Vanilla yogurt

Quick Substitutes When You Run Out:

1 tablespoon prepared mustard .... 1 teaspoon dry mustard

1 slice bread .... ½ cup bread crumbs

1 teaspoon dry herbs .... 1 teaspoon fresh herbs

1 cup uncooked rice .... 3 cups cooked rice

1 clove garlic .... ⅛ teaspoon garlic powder

1 square chocolate .... 3 tablespoons cocoa +
1 teaspoon butter or margarine

1 cup buttermilk .... 1 cup milk + 1 tablespoon lemon
juice or vinegar, stirred in

3 medium bananas .... 1 cup mashed banana

10 miniature marshmallows .... 1 large marshmallow

1 tablespoon cornstarch (for thickening) .... 2 tablespoons all-purpose flour

1 teaspoon baking powder .... ¼ teaspoon baking soda
½ teaspoon cream of tartar

Try These Healthier Substitutes:

1 cup heavy cream .... 1 cup evaporated skimmed milk

1 cup sour cream .... 1 cup fat free sour cream or fat
free plain yogurt

1 (8-ounce) package cream cheese .... 1 (8-ounce) package fat free
cream cheese

1 cup shredded cheese .... 1 cup reduced fat shredded
cheese

1 egg .... 2 egg whites

1 ounce baking chocolate .... 3 tablespoons cocoa +
1 tablespoon canola oil

Apple Casserole .... 1.5 other carb., 2 fruit

Artichoke and Onion Couscous .... 2 starch, 1 vegetable

Asparagus with Lemon Caper Vinaigrette ...... 1 vegetable

Avocado Cucumber Soup .... 1 vegetable, 1 fat

Baked Beans .... 1.5 starch, 1 other carb., 1.5 very
lean meat, 0.5 vegetable

Banana Bread .... 1 starch, 1 other carb., 0.5 fruit, 1 fat

Banana Pie with Chocolate Glaze .... 1.5 starch, 1 other carb., 1 fruit,
1.5 fat

Banana Pudding Trifle .... 1 starch, 1 other carb., 0.5 fruit,
0.5 fat

Banana Split Pie .... 2 other carb., 0.5 fruit, 0.5 fat

Barbecued Brisket .... 0.5 other carb., 5.5 very lean meat,
1 fat

Barley and Mushroom Casserole .... 1.5 starch

Basic Barley .... 1.5 starch

Basic Risotto .... 3 starch, 0.5 very lean meat,
0.5 fat

Basil Chicken .... 0.5 starch, 3.5 very lean meat

Berry French Toast .... 2 starch, 1 other carb., 0.5 fruit

Best Black and White Bean Spread .... 0.5 starch

Best Blueberry Muffins .... 1 starch, 0.5 other carb., 1 fat

Black Bean and
Caramelized Onion Burritos .... 2 starch, 1 very lean meat,
1 vegetable, 0.5 fat

Black Bean and Corn Salad .... 1 starch, 0.5 very lean meat,
1 vegetable, 1 fat

Black Bean and Corn Salsa .... 0.5 starch

Black Bean Chili .... 2 starch, 1.5 vegetable

Black-Eyed Pea Salad .... 1.5 starch, 1 vegetable, 1 fat

Black-Eyed Pea Salsa .... 1 vegetable

Blueberry Bundt Cake .... 1 starch, 1.5 other carb., 1 fat

Blueberry Pineapple Delight .... 2 other carb., 0.5 fruit, 1.5 fat

Bran Muffins .... 1 starch, 0.5 other carb., 0.5 fat

Bread Pudding Florentine .... 1.5 starch, 1.5 very lean meat,
1 vegetable, 1 fat

Breakfast Bake with Spanish Sauce .... 0.5 other carb., 1 very lean meat,
1 vegetable, 0.5 fat

Broccoli and Cauliflower Salad .... 1 vegetable, 0.5 fat

Broccoli and Cauliflower
with Garlic Cheese Sauce .... 0.5 very lean meat, 1 vegetable

Broccoli Casserole .... 0.5 starch, 0.5 very lean meat,
1.5 vegetable

Broccoli Corn Mini Muffins .... 0.5 starch

Broccoli Salad .... 0.5 other carb., 0.5 vegetable, 0.5 fat

Buttermilk Brownies .... 1 other carb., 1 fat

Caesar Salad .... 0.5 vegetable, 1 fat

Carrot Cake .... 0.5 starch, 1 other carb., 1 fat

Cheese Stuffed Manicotti .... 2 lean meat, 3 vegetables

Cheesy Eggplant Casserole .... 1 starch, 0.5 lean meat, 3.5 vegetable

Chewy Fruity Blonde Brownies .... 0.5 other carb., 0.5 fat

Chicken and Broccoli .... 2 starch, 4 very lean meat, 3 vegetable, 0.5 fat

Chicken and Wild Rice Casserole .... 2 starch, 3.5 very lean meat, 1 vegetable

Chicken Caesar Sandwich .... 1.5 starch, 2 very lean meat, 0.5 fat

Chicken Elegante .... 3.5 very lean meat, 1 vegetable, 0.5 fat

Chicken Enchilada Casserole .... 1.5 starch, 2.5 very lean meat, 1 fat

Chicken Piccata .... 0.5 starch, 3.5 very lean meat, 1 fat

Chicken Rice Medley .... 2.5 starch, 4 very lean meat

Chicken Rosemary Strips .... 1.5 very lean meat

Chicken Salad .... 0.5 starch, 2 very lean meat, 0.5 fruit, 0.5 vegetable

Chicken Tortilla Soup .... 1.5 starch, 2 very lean meat, 2 vegetable

Chicken Vermicelli .... 1.5 starch, 2.5 very lean meat, 1 vegetable

Chicken with Black Bean Sauce .... 0.5 starch, 4 very lean meat, 1 vegetable

Chicken with Tomato Tarragon Sauce .... 3.5 very lean meat, 1.5 vegetable

Chili Boats .... 0.5 starch

Chili Cheese Bread .... 1 starch

Coffee Punch .... 1 other carb.

Corn and Wild Rice Soup .... 2.5 starch, 0.5 very lean meat, 0.5 vegetable

Cornbread .... 1 starch, 0.5 fat

Cornbread and Rice Dressing .... 1 starch, 0.5 very lean meat, 0.5 vegetable

Corny Rice .... 2.5 starch

Couscous Salad .... 1 starch, 0.5 vegetable, 0.5 fat

Crab and Avocado Mold .... 1 very lean meat, 0.5 fat

Crab Cakes with
    Horseradish and Caper Sauce .... 1 starch, 1.5 very lean meat, 0.5 fat

Cranberry and White
  Chocolate Chip Cookies .... 1 starch, 0.5 fat
Cranberry and White Chocolate Treats .... 0.5 other carb., 0.5 fat
Cranberry Orange Bundt Cake .... 1 starch, 1 other carb., 1 fat
Cranberry Yam Bread .... 1 starch, 1 other carb., 1 fat
Cream of Spinach and Sweet Potato Soup ...... 2 starch, 1 very lean meat,
  1.5 vegetable
Creamed Double Potatoes .... 2 starch, 0.5 fat
Creamy Potato Soup .... 1 starch, 0.5 very lean meat,
  0.5 vegetable, 0.5 fat
Easy Pot Roast .... 5 very lean meat, 1 vegetable, 1 fat
Easy Strawberry Custard Cake .... 1 starch, 1 other carb., 1 fat
Egg and Green Chili Casserole .... 2 starch, 2 very lean meat, 2 fat
Eggplant Bake with Beef .... 1.5 starch, 2 very lean meat,
  1 vegetable, 1 fat
Espresso Brownies .... 0.5 other carb., 0.5 fat
Fish with Horseradish Mustard Sauce .... 2 very lean meat
Frosty Strawberry Soup .... 1 other carb., 1 fruit
Fruit Crumble .... 1 starch, 1 other carb., 1 fruit, 1 fat
Fruit Salsa Quesadillas .... 2.5 starch, 0.5 lean meat,
  0.5 fruit, 0.5 fat
Glazed Pork Roast
  with Maple-Mustard Sauce .... 1 other carb., 1.5 very lean meat,
  0.5 fat
Glazed Pork Tenderloins .... 1 other carb., 3.5 very lean meat
Glazed Salmon with Cantaloupe Salsa .... 0.5 other carb., 3 lean meat, 1 fat
Great Greek Chicken .... 4 very lean meat, 1 vegetable, 1 fat
Greek Pasta Salad .... 2 starch, 1 vegetable
Greek Shrimp Bake .... 0.5 starch, 3.5 very lean meat,
  1 vegetable, 1 fat
Heavenly Yam Delight .... 0.5 starch, 1 other carb., 1 fat
Herbed Carrots .... 1 vegetable, 0.5 fat
Holiday Rice Pilaf .... 2.5 starch, 0.5 very lean meat,
  0.5 vegetable, 1 fat
Italian Pizza Slices .... 1 starch
Italian Pork Chops .... 4 very lean meat,
  0.5 vegetable, 2 fat
Italian Puffs .... 1 starch, 1 fat
Italian Shrimp and Pasta .... 2 starch, 3.5 very lean meat, 0.5 fat
Lamb Stew .... 3.5 lean meat, 2 vegetable
Lemon Cheesecake
  with Raspberry Sauce .... 0.5 starch, 1 very lean meat, 0.5 fat
Lemon Ice .... 1.5 other carb., 0.5 skim milk

Lemon Raspberry Bread .... 1 starch, 1 other carb., 1 fat

Lemon Sweet Potato Casserole .... 2.5 starch, 1 other carb., 0.5 fat

Mango Soup .... 0.5 other carb., 1.5 fruit

Maple Dijon Glazed Turkey Breast .... 0.5 other carb., 4 very lean meat

Marinated Shrimp .... 0.5 very lean meat

Marinated Tuna with Pineapple Salsa .... 4.5 lean meat, 1 fruit, 0.5 vegetable

Mediterranean Red Snapper .... 4 very lean meat, 1 vegetable, 1 fat

Mexican Lasagne .... 1 starch, 2 lean meat, 1 vegetable

Mexican Layered Dip .... 0.5 fat

Mushroom Barley Soup .... 1 starch, 1 very lean meat,
2 vegetable

Oatmeal Crunch Cookies .... 0.5 starch, 0.5 other carb., 0.5 fat

Orange and Walnut Green Salad .... 0.5 vegetable, 1 fat

Orange Raspberry Ice Cream Dessert .... 1.5 other carb., 1 fruit

Oven Fried Chicken .... 1.5 starch, 3.5 very lean meat,
0.5 fat

Pan Smoked Salmon Southwestern Style ..... 4 lean meat, 1 fat

Parmesan Chicken Pasta .... 3 starch, 3.5 very lean meat,
1 vegetable, 1 fat

Pasta with Black Beans .... 3.5 starch, 1 very lean meat,
1 vegetable, 0.5 fat

Pasta with Broccoli and Beans .... 4.5 starch, 0.5 very lean meat,
1.5 vegetable, 0.5 fat

Peach Cake .... 1 starch, 2 other carb., 1 fat

Peachy Upside Down Cake .... 0.5 starch, 1 other carb., 1 fat

Pesto Pasta .... 3 starch, 1 vegetable, 2 fat

Pistachio Marble Cake .... 3 other carb., 1 fat

Poppyseed Pasta .... 2 starch, 0.5 fat

Pork Stew .... 5 very lean meat, 0.5 fruit,
2 vegetable, 0.5 fat

Potato Pizza .... 1 starch, 0.5 fat

Quick Veggie Soup .... 1 starch, 2 vegetable

Rice and Bean Salad .... 1.5 starch

Rice and Pasta Blend .... 2 starch, 0.5 fat

Rice Primavera .... 1 starch, 1 vegetable

Risotto with Artichokes .... 2.5 starch, 1 vegetable

Roasted Pepper and Spinach Penne .... 4 starch, 1.5 vegetable, 2 fat

Roasted Potatoes and Onions .... 1.5 starch, 0.5 vegetable, 1 fat

Roasted Red Pepper
and Mushroom Polenta Pizza .... 0.5 starch

Salsa Chicken .... 4 very lean meat, 0.5 vegetable,
0.5 fat

Salsa Lasagne .... 1.5 starch, 2 very lean meat,
1 vegetable, 1 fat

Sautéed Mushrooms .... 1 vegetable, 0.5 fat

Scalloped Potatoes .... 2.5 starch

Scallops with Black Beans .... 0.5 starch, 3 very lean meat

Seafood Toast .... 0.5 starch, 0.5 very lean meat

Shrimp and Spinach Pasta Toss .... 3 starch, 3.5 very lean meat,
0.5 vegetable, 1 fat

Shrimp Boat .... 1 starch, 1 very lean meat

Shrimp Casserole .... 1.5 starch, 3.5 very lean meat

Shrimp Enchiladas .... 3 starch, 2 very lean meat,
0.5 vegetable, 1 fat

Shrimp Fettuccine .... 2 starch, 3.5 very lean meat,
1 vegetable

Shrimp Pear Pasta Salad .... 2 bread, 1 very lean meat,
0.5 fruit, 0.5 vegetable

Shrimp Peppers and Cheese Grits .... 1 starch, 4 very lean meat,
0.5 vegetable

Shrimp Salsa .... 0.5 very lean meat, 0.5 vegetable

Shrimp Soft Tacos with Cranberry Salsa .... 2 starch, 2.5 very lean meat,
0.5 fruit, 0.5 vegetable, 1 fat

Shrimp Stir Fry with Toasted Pecans .... 3.5 very lean meat, 1 vegetable,
0.5 fat

Shrimp, Asparagus and Brie Pasta .... 3 starch, 4 very lean meat,
0.5 vegetable, 1 fat

Simply Salmon Pasta .... 2 starch, 1 lean meat, 1.5 vegetable,
0.5 fat

Slice and Bake Chocolate Chip Cookies .... 0.5 other carb., 0.5 fat

Smashed Potatoes .... 2 starch, 1 fat

Southwestern Chicken Salad .... 0.5 starch, 1.5 very lean meat,
0.5 vegetable

Southwestern Chicken Soup .... 1 starch, 3.5 very lean meat,
1 vegetable, 1 fat

Southwestern Cracked Wheat Salad .... 2 starch, 0.5 very lean meat,
0.5 vegetable

Southwestern Pasta .... 3 starch, 1 vegetable, 1 fat

Southwestern Spinach Lasagne .... 2 starch, 1 very lean meat,
1 vegetable, 1.5 fat

Sparkling Pineapple Lemonade .... 0.5 other carb., 1 fruit

Spicy Tea Punch .... 1 other carb., 1 fruit

Spicy Topped Trout .... 3.5 very lean meat, 1.5 fat

Spinach and Artichoke Casserole .... 2 vegetable, 0.5 skim milk, 1 fat

Spinach and Corn Casserole .... 1.5 starch, 1 vegetable, 0.5 fat

Spinach and Tomato Crustless Quiche .... 2 very lean meat, 1.5 vegetable, 1 fat

Spinach Dip .... Free

Spinach Lasagne .... 1 starch, 2 lean meat, 2 vegetables, 1 fat

Spinach Toast .... 1 starch, 0.5 vegetable

Spinach Tortellini Salad .... 3 vegetable, 1 fat

Strawberry and Kiwi Mixed Green Salad
  with Poppy-Sesame Dressing .... 1 fruit, 1 vegetable, 1 fat

Strawberry Bread .... 1 starch, 1 other carb., 1 fat

Strawberry Cheesecake Squares .... 0.5 starch, 0.5 fruit, 0.5 fat

Strawberry Fruit Dip .... Free

Stuffed Chicken Breasts
  with Enchilada Sauce .... 1 starch, 4 very lean meat, 0.5 vegetable, 0.5 skim milk, 1 fat

Stuffed Flounder Florentine .... 3.5 very lean meat, 1 vegetable

Stuffed Potatoes Primavera .... 2 starch, 1 lean meat, 2 vegetable, 1.5 fat

Stuffed Tenderloin .... 4.5 very lean meat, 1.5 fat

Summer Squash Casserole .... 0.5 starch, 1 vegetable, 0.5 skim milk

Summer Veggie Pasta .... 3 starch, 1.5 vegetable, 1 fat

Sun-Dried Tomato Bread .... 1 starch, 0.5 very lean meat, 0.5 vegetable, 1 fat

Super Salsa .... 0.5 vegetable, 0.5 fat

Super Snapper .... 0.5 starch, 3.5 very lean meat

Super Tossed Salad .... 0.5 vegetable, 0.5 fat

Sweet Potato and Apple Soup .... 2.5 starch, 0.5 very lean meat, 0.5 fruit

Sweet Potato Cranberry Galette .... 2 starch, 0.5 fruit, 1 fat

Sweet Potato Pancakes
  with Apple Walnut Topping .... 1 starch, 0.5 other carb.

Sweet Potato Pecan Pie .... 1 starch, 3 other carb., 2.5 fat

Sweet Potato Salad .... 2.5 starch, 0.5 vegetable, 1 fat

Sweet Potato, Apple, and Walnut Muffins ...... 1 starch, 0.5 other carb., 0.5 fat

Tabouleh Salad .... 1 starch, 0.5 vegetable

Taco Soup .... 2 starch, 3.5 very lean meat, 1 vegetable, 1 fat

Tasty Beef Strips .... 3.5 starch, 4.5 very lean meat, 0.5 vegetable, 0.5 fat

Tortellini Primavera .... 2.5 starch, 1 lean meat, 3 vegetable, 0.5 skim milk, 0.5 fat

Triple Corn Pudding .... 2.5 starch, 1 fat

Tropical Couscous Salad .... 2 starch, 1 fruit, 0.5 fat

Tropical Fruit Gazpacho .... 1 fruit, 0.5 vegetable

Tropical Fruity Cheese Spread .... 0.5 very lean meat

Trout Amandine .... 0.5 starch, 3.5 very lean meat, 1.5 fat

Tuna and Barley Niçoise .... 1 starch, 3.5 very lean meat, 1 vegetable, 1 fat

Tuna Pasta Salad .... 1 starch, 1.5 very lean meat, 0.5 vegetable, 0.5 fat

Twice Baked Yams .... 1.5 starch, 0.5 other carb., 1 fruit

Ultimate Cheesecake .... 1 starch, 1 other carb., 1.5 very lean meat, 1 fat

Ultimate Coconut Cake .... 3.5 other carb., 0.5 fat

Ultimate Green Salad with Balsamic Vinaigrette:
  Salad .... 0.5 fruit, 1 fat
  Balsamic Vinaigrette .... 1 other carb., 1 fat

Ultimate Red Pasta Sauce .... 4 vegetable

Veal Roll Ups .... 0.5 starch, 5.5 very lean meat, 0.5 vegetable, 1 fat

Veal Scaloppine .... 4 very lean meat, 1 vegetable, 1 fat

Veal, Mushroom and Broccoli
  with Tomato Vinaigrette .... 2.5 starch, 5 very lean meat, 1 vegetable, 1.5 fat

Veggie Au Gratin .... 2.5 starch, 1 very lean meat, 1.5 vegetable

Veggie Couscous .... 2 starch, 0.5 vegetable, 0.5 fat

Veggie Paella .... 3 starch, 0.5 very lean meat, 0.5 vegetable, 0.5 fat

Very Good Vermicelli .... 2.5 starch, 0.5 fat

White Chocolate and Strawberry Trifle .... 1 starch, 2 other carb., 1 fruit, 0.5 milk, 0.5 fat

White Chocolate Bundt Cake
  with Raspberry Sauce .... 3 other carb., 0.5 fruit, 1.5 fat

White Spinach Pizza .... 1 starch, 0.5 vegetable

Wild Rice and Mushroom Soup .... 1 starch, 0.5 very lean meat, 1 vegetable

Wild Rice and Pea Casserole .... 1 starch, 0.5 vegetable

Wild Rice Stuffing .... 2 starch, 0.5 very lean meat, 1 fruit, 0.5 fat

Wonderful White Chili with Tomato Salsa ...... 1.5 starch, 2.5 very lean meat, 0.5 vegetable

Yam Biscuits .... 1 starch

Yam Cranberry Bundt Cake .... 3 starch, 1 fat

Index

INDEX

INDEX

INDEX

HOLLY B. CLEGG
13431 Woodmont Court
Baton Rouge, Louisiana 70810-5334

Please send me the following copies:

Meals On The Move: Rush Hour Recipes _____ copies @ $19.95 = _____

A Trim and Terrific Louisiana Kitchen:
   Southern Cuisine _____ copies @ $18.95 = _____

Trim & Terrific American Favorites _____ copies @ $18.95 = _____

Trim & Terrific One Dish Favorites _____ copies @ $18.95 = _____

SUBTOTAL $ _____

(Louisiana residents add 8.94% sales tax) **TAX** _____

POSTAGE AND HANDLING ($4.00) _____

Postage and handling for each additional book ($1.00) _____

TOTAL $ _____

Name _____

Address _____

City _____ State _____ Zip Code _____

Telephone Number (_____) _____

Please charge to my ☐ Mastercard ☐ Visa

Card # _____ Expiration Date_____

Signature of Cardholder _____
OR CHARGE BY PHONE **1-800-88HOLLY**

Make checks payable to Holly B. Clegg

Visit my website: HollyClegg.com